THE
POTTER'S
PRIMER

THE POTTER'S PRIMER

by Eleanor Chroman

HAWTHORN BOOKS, INC.
Publishers/New York

738.

THE POTTER'S PRIMER

Library of Congress Catalog Card Number: 73-11741

ISBN: 0-8015-5958-8

First Printing, May 1974
Second Printing, October 1974
Third Printing, August 1975
Fourth Printing, February 1976
Fifth Printing, January 1977

For Pete,
whose hand was always
there when I needed it

Contents

ACKNOWLEDGMENTS xiii

1 POTTERY: AN ANCIENT FUNCTIONAL ART FORM 1

2 GETTING TO KNOW THE MEDIUM 15
CERAMICS VERSUS POTTERY 15
THE NATURE OF THE MEDIUM 15
WHERE DOES IT COME FROM? 16
TYPES OF CLAYS 17
NATURAL CLAY VERSUS CLAY BODIES 17
SOME CLAY BODIES 19
  Porcelain 19
  Earthenware 19
  Stoneware 20

3 GETTING THE CLAY—TO BUY OR NOT TO BUY 21
DIGGING YOUR OWN CLAY 21
BUYING CLAY 24
  How to Buy—Wet or Dry? 25
  Some Things to Consider When Buying Clay 26

4 BEFORE YOU BEGIN 27
MATERIALS 28
PREPARING THE CLAY 30
  Mixing Dry Clay 30
WEDGING 31
  Method I 32
  Method II 34
RECONDITIONING THE CLAY 35
STORING 35
GROG 36
DRYING 37
FIRING AND GLAZING 39

5 GETTING THE "FEEL" OF THINGS 40

    EXERCISES IN MANIPULATION 40
    EXERCISES IN TEXTURE 41

6 SIMPLE CLAY PROJECTS 43

    BEADS 43
    BUTTONS 45
    JEWELRY 47
        Pendants, Pins, and Earrings 47
        Necklaces 49
    TILES 51
    TRIVETS 55
    HANGING PIECES—MOBILES AND WIND CHIMES 56

7 PINCH POTS 59

    BASIC PINCH POTS 60
    BOWLS, ASHTRAYS, AND VASES 62
        Bowls 63
        Ashtrays 63
        Vases 64
    BELLS 66
    GARDEN GOBLINS 69
    PINCH POT ANIMALS 71
        Small Pinch Pot Turtle 72

8 COIL POTS 74

    BASIC COIL POTS—CYLINDERS 76
    BOWLS AND VASES 79
        Bowls 80
        Templates 81
        Vases 82
    LARGE POTS 83
    PIECES WITH HANDLES 84
        Coiled Handles 85

9 SLAB POTS 87

    SLAB TRAYS OR PLATES 89
    SLING PIECES—PLATTER 91
        Sling Pieces 93
    BOXES 95
    FREE-FORM CONSTRUCTIONS 98
    DOWEL ROD TECHNIQUE 102

10 DO-IT-YOURSELF MOLDS 106

   USING NEWSPAPERS 107
      Hanging Weed Pot 107
      Three-dimensional Mask 110
   USING PAPER TUBES 112
   USING OATMEAL BOXES 114
   USING MIXING BOWLS 115
      Coiled Bowls or Hanging Planter 115
   USING BOTTLES 118

11 NON-FIRE CLAYS 121

   OVEN-FIRE PRODUCTS 122
      Steps in Using Oven-Fire Clays 123
   SELF-HARDENING PRODUCTS 124
   COOKIE-CUTTER CHRISTMAS TREE ORNAMENTS 125

12 THE POTTER'S WHEEL 127

   GENERAL INFORMATION 127
   CLAY FOR THROWING 131
   TOOLS 132
   BASIC TIPS 133
   TEN STEPS FOR THROWING 135
   MAKING A CYLINDER 136
   TRIMMING 141
   MAKING A BOWL 143
   MAKING A BOTTLE 144
   TRIMMING A BOTTLE 146
   LIPS AND RIMS 149
   THROWING "OFF THE HUMP" 150

13 ACCOUTREMENTS TO WHEEL THROWING 152

   PULLING HANDLES 152
      Variations 155
   MAKING A PITCHER 156
   THROWING A LID 157
   MAKING A CASSEROLE 157
   KNOBS 158
   SPOUTS 160

14 VARYING THE BASIC WHEEL FORM 163

   WHEEL-THROWN OWL 163
   THROWN PIGGY BANK 165
   SECTIONAL CONSTRUCTIONS 166

15 DECORATING TECHNIQUES—PRE-FIRING 168

    PROCESSES USED ON WET CLAY 169
      Impressed Decorations 170
      Adding Clay 172
    PROCESSES USED ON LEATHER-HARD CLAY 172
      Carving 172
      Appliqués 173
      Slip Decoration 174
        Coating 174
        Painting 174
        Slip Trailing 176
        Sgraffito 178
    DECORATING ON DRY CLAY 179

16 GLAZING 181

    THE FUNCTION OF GLAZE 181
    GLAZE COMPOSITION 181
    COMMERCIAL GLAZES 182
    HOW TO CHOOSE GLAZES 183
    TEST TILES 185
    STEPS PRECEDING GLAZING 186
    METHODS OF GLAZING 187
      Brushing 187
      Pouring 189
      Dipping 191
      Spraying 192
    GLAZE DECORATION 193
      Engobes 194
      Sgraffito 194
      Wax Resist 195
      Oxides or Stains 195
      Frit 199
      Luster Decoration 200
    EGYPTIAN PASTE 203
    COMMON GLAZE FLAWS 207

17 FIRING 209

    PROCESSES PRECEDING FIRING 210
    KILNS—GENERAL INFORMATION 210
    REDUCTION-FIRING 211
    CONES 214
    KILN FURNITURE 216
    LOADING THE KILN 217

FIRING BEADS   218
FIRING THE KILN   219
RAKU   220
   Making Raku Pottery   222

EPILOGUE   225
GLOSSARY   228
INDEX   233

Acknowledgments

No book of this nature is ever the creation of one person. There are many people who have given of their time and talents and whose contributions have influenced the pages between these covers.

Special thanks must go to my mother, Anne Gregory, whose help in so many ways made the difficult more possible.

I am indebted to Larry Mosher and Michi Zimmerman for reading this manuscript; to Monika Guiteras for her beautiful drawings; to Eunice Prieto for her kindness and generosity in allowing me to photograph Anthony Prieto's pottery and giving me access to the Mills Collection; to the Rosicrucian Egyptian Museum for the lovely photographs they contributed to this book; to Howard Berliant, Margaret d'Hamer, Clayton Baylie, and Jon Manheim for the use of their photographs; and to the many artists and friends who lent me their pieces for inclusion in this book—especially to Anni Grundler and Michele Cole, as well as Michi Zimmerman, Andrée Thompson, Peggy King, Donna Oestreich, Joanne Sommerville, Diana Bohn, Deborah Kaufman, and others. I particularly want to thank Judy and Mike Bursak of the Hearthstone Potter for their cooperation on the chapters on throwing, which feature Judy's ceramic talents.

And last I want to thank the many friends whose encouragement, patience, and excellent suggestions added invaluably to this book.

THE
POTTER'S
PRIMER

1

POTTERY: AN ANCIENT FUNCTIONAL ART FORM

Man's relationship with clay goes back to his earliest beginnings. Through the centuries, from the dawn of civilization to the space age, it has served his needs both as a functional and creative medium. When prehistoric man discovered that the soft mud-like substance he found along a river bank hardened in the hot sun, he learned to shape it with his hands into rough bowls. Now he had containers in which to collect and store the nuts and berries that he gathered. Or perhaps he used clay first to seal baskets that he had made from rough fibers and found that when this lining dried, it could be used sans basket as a useful receptacle of its own. After he learned to use fire, he discovered, probably by accident, that his clay ware, when submitted to high heat, not only withstood the fire but in fact emerged far more durable. While the rains would melt it back to mud before it was put into the fire, the high heat made it permanently hard. Now it would, at least temporarily, hold water and could be used for cooking as well as storing. This important discovery gave early man greater control in providing for his most basic need—food. Since that time pottery has paralleled the course of human history.

As man's existence became more than a mere struggle for survival, he began to see the world not only as a hostile environment but also as a place where great beauty existed. His eyes opened to the wonders of nature, and as civilization advanced he sought to create beauty himself. He felt a great need to feed his spirit as well as his belly. He began to pay attention to form as well as function. To make not only a bowl, but a bowl that was pleasing to the senses. He learned to paint designs on his pots with colored clays and to use materials from nature, such as bark, shells, pebbles, pods, and sticks to imprint its wet surface and thus vary the clay's smooth texture.

With the invention of the wheel, the potter's wheel came into existence. The same round shape that enabled man to make the cart, wagon, and chariot also made the manufacture of clay ware much faster and easier. Over 5,000 years ago, the ancient Sumerians were already proficient in its use.

Glazing was also discovered thousands of years ago, and it added a whole new dimension to finished clay products. (Fragments of glaze ware as old as 3,000 B.C. have been discovered in Egyptian tombs.) At last, man was able to make his pots nonporous—to coat them with a glasslike substance that enabled him to store liquids without having them leak through the container. Not only did glazes provide a sealer to make pottery watertight, they also opened up new possibilities of color and design. Now not only was a piece of pottery useful, but its potential as a thing of beauty was greatly increased.

Man learned that clay had many uses. He made bricks by mixing it with straw. He made tiles to decorate his walls and buildings. The first written documents of recorded history were set down on clay tablets—soft slabs of clay marked with sharp instruments—perhaps a bit cumbersome, but nevertheless permanent. Many of our records of early cultures have been handed down in this form. The early Egyptians used a clay-glaze compound called faience, or Egyptian paste, to make beautiful jewelry and figures of gods and animals. In many early civilizations pottery evolved into a highly developed art form.

Pottery, one of the oldest crafts, has changed and grown concurrently with man's development. From the first rough bowl of the Stone Age to the complex contemporary field of ceramics, clay has served man as a utilitarian and artistic medium. Since the early Egyptians fashioned earthenware pots as long as 10,000 years ago, the craft of pottery has undergone tremendous changes. Today, a variety of clays, glazes, tools, wheels, and kilns are available, providing almost unlimited possibilities for the creator. Yet the result of the finished product primarily depends, as it has through the ages, upon the skill of the potter's hands.

In today's specialized, technological society, many of us have lost touch with the work of our own hands and the pride that creation provides. Crafts are enjoying a renaissance at this time, and we have a chance to recapture the satisfaction that the artisans of the past enjoyed in their work.

This blacktopped red pottery, found in the early and middle predynastic period, is the earliest form of pottery found in Egyptian civilization. It is entirely handmade, as the wheel was not invented until about the first dynasty. The blacktop was probably obtained by placing the pottery down in the hot ashes of a fire. It is 5½ inches high. (Photo courtesy of the Rosicrucian Egyptian Museum, San Jose, California)

Ancient Egyptian clay jars for children. These rare jars are made in the form of Bes, the god of dancing, music, and gaiety. They were found at Heliopolis. Each is 4¼ inches high. (Photo courtesy of the Rosicrucian Egyptian Museum)

Painted pottery face of funereal tomb figure from Egypt.
This portion of the sculpture is 2¼ inches high. (*Photo
courtesy of the Rosicrucian Egyptian Museum*)

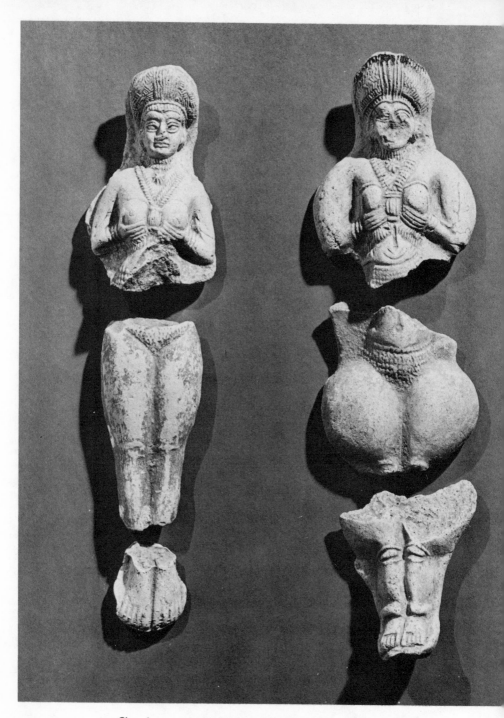

Clay fragments of "Mother Goddess" figures from Marlik
(present-day Iran). These are from a culture that existed
in the second and third millennium B.C. (*Photo courtesy
of the Rosicrucian Egyptian Museum*)

Clay tablet from the ruins of a temple in the ancient city of Lagash. It dates back to the rule of Entemena, one of the early Babylonian kings. Inscribed in one of the earliest forms of Babylonian writing called Early Linear Babylonian Script. The translation tells us Entemena built a temple to E-Ninni, one of the gods of the Ancient Sumerians. Before 3,000 B.C. Measures 9 by 11½ by 2¼ inches. (*Photo courtesy of the Rosicrucian Egyptian Museum*)

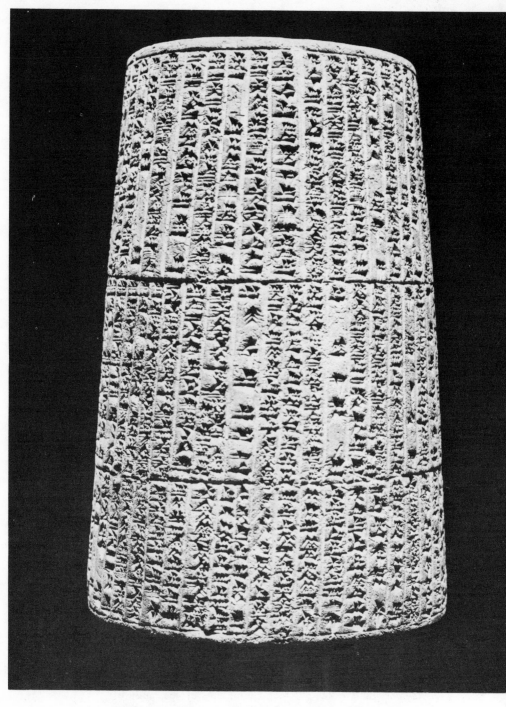

Babylonian pottery barrel cylinder proclamation by Nebuchadnezzar II. Measures 8¼ inches high. (Photo courtesy of the Rosicrucian Egyptian Museum)

Female figurine. This Cypriote terra-cotta statuette is from the Late Bronze Age, around 1500 B.C. This type of figurine, which recalls representations of the goddess Ishtar on Babylonian cylinder seals, is thought to be of Oriental inspiration. It occurs not only in Cyprus but in Egypt, Syria, and in other parts of western Asia. This figure is 21 centimeters tall. (Lowie Museum of Anthropology, University of California, Berkeley)

Attic geometric jug. Not one of the largest of the colossal trefoil jugs of classical Dipylon ware, but one of the best in shape. Severely geometric in design. Ninth to eighth century B.C. This jug is 67 centimeters tall. (Lowie Museum of Anthropology, University of California, Berkeley)

Female figurine. This skirted figure of a woman holding
a jar in her hand dates back to 750 to 1,000 A.D. It
comes from Mexico, from the Nayarit, Ixtlan del Rio
area. It is 16½ centimeters high. (*Lowie Museum of Anthropology, University of California, Berkeley*)

Chinese tomb figurine. T'ang Dynasty, eighth century
A.D. Court lady on galloping horse. Buff pottery with
traces of white, vermilion, orange, black, and gray-
green pigments. This figure measures 38 centimeters high
with stand. (*Lowie Museum of Anthropology, University
of California, Berkeley*)

Clay is a wonderful medium—a way of getting in touch with oneself through the ancient relationship of man with earth and fire. Here we have the opportunity to take a formless lump of pliable earth and, through the use of our hands and the creative forces working within each of us, convert it into a durable finished form uniquely our own. Every step of the way, from blob to bowl, the clay belongs to us. The finished product is as flexible as the material itself—limited only by our own skill and imagination.

If you are reading this book, you are already interested in clay. It is the hope of the author that this volume will encourage the growth of that interest and, through the means of simple and successful experiences in the medium, build up the newcomer's confidence to progress further on his own. No book can take the place of the face-to-face relationship with a good teacher. Once clay has cast its spell on you—as it will if you continue with it—you will arrive at the point where you will find it necessary to take some instruction. Almost any geographical area has recreation departments, adult schools, community centers, college courses, as well as private workshops and schools that give classes in both hand-building and wheel-throwing. Once you have gone through all the projects in this book or while you are still working on them, a class in pottery will greatly expand your skill and enhance your progress. Whether you choose pottery as a hobby or a career, it will provide you with many happy hours of getting back in tune with some of the basic qualities within you. From blob to bowl— the experience is yours to enjoy.

Equestrian figurine. This Cypriote terra-cotta statuette probably dates from the seventh to the sixth century B.C. The long neck and stiff mane of the horse are characteristic of the period. Black and red ornamentation represents, in part, horse trappings. The figurine is 15½ centimeters tall. (*Lowie Museum of Anthropology, University of California, Berkeley*)

Pitcher with missing handle. This intricately designed piece dates back to 625 to 600 B.C. It comes from Greece from the area of Corinth. It is only 7 centimeters high yet embellished with a goose between two heraldic sphinxes and a lion, as well as rosettes and a Greek key pattern on the lip. (*Lowie Museum of Anthropology, University of California, Berkeley*)

Middle Corinthian column krater. Black figure with red infusions, showing a battle scene. It dates back to 597 to 590 B.C. It is 29 centimeters high. (*Lowie Museum of Anthropology, University of California, Berkeley*)

Goblet painted with men carrying spear-throwers and bundles of spears. It comes from Nasca, Peru, about 250 A.D. It is 16½ centimeters high. (*Lowie Museum of Anthropology, University of California, Berkeley*)

13

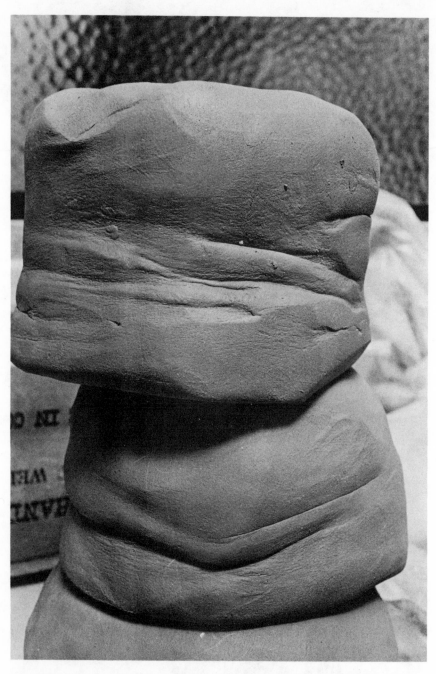

Moist clay ready for use. (Photograph by Howard M. Berliant)

CERAMICS VERSUS POTTERY

2

GETTING TO KNOW THE MEDIUM

Before we begin a discussion of clay, let us clear up one of the questions that is so often asked by newcomers. "What is the difference—or is there one—between pottery and ceramics?" These terms are often used interchangeably, sometimes correctly, sometimes incorrectly. Ceramics is the entire art (or craft) of making products from the raw materials of the earth and subjecting them to fire. Pottery is part of ceramics. It is not *all* of ceramics; ceramics also includes enameling on various metals; glass-, brick-, and tile-making; and such commercial productions as the making of clay pipe and porcelain fixtures. While your bathtub may be a ceramic object, it can hardly be said to be a piece of pottery. While it is correct to say that pottery is a branch of ceramics, the converse is not true. So—you may call your clay products either pottery or ceramics. Both terms are correct. But, when you speak of ceramics, you are referring to a complex field. When you speak of pottery, you are referring to a specialized craft.

THE NATURE OF THE MEDIUM

Clay is a plastic material. When it has the right consistency—neither too wet nor too dry—it can be shaped into an infinite variety of forms. The main and only really indispensable tools required for its shaping are the potter's hands. Other tools, while not essential, add to the refinements of the finished product.

In its plastic state, clay can be pounded, squeezed, coiled, pinched, thrown, and manipulated into a variety of shapes to attain the form the potter wishes it to hold. As it dries, it becomes hard and shrinks.

At this point the clay is still reusable. If the finished product does not turn out as you envisioned, the clay can be broken up and reconstituted to be used again in future projects. Once the clay has been fired, however, it becomes permanently hard. From that time on, for better or for worse, the piece is yours. When the clay is fired, it shrinks again. The bowl that seemed so enormous upon creation not only *seems* to have shrunk by stages (first in drying, then in firing), it has actually done so—becoming, perhaps in contrast, not quite as impressive in size as originally planned.

Clay in its pliable state provides great freedom and variety in its manipulation. But, because of this very plasticity, it also has its limitations. Forms that are too extreme—too tall, too thin, with too many long slender projections—tend to collapse while they are still wet. Because clay becomes brittle when it is fired, long thin extensions tend to break off. When these are glazed, they become extremely dangerous since the glossy coating adds a knifelike sharpness to the long, thin, now glasslike projections. They could easily cut hands that touch them. Since pottery is a tactile as well as a visual art form, this would not be in keeping with the basic qualities of the medium.

Clay is a simple material with its own special characteristics. The charm of the hand-crafted pot lies in the fact that it is just that—a piece of pottery with a special look and feel uniquely its own, an object created by the potter's hands with the aid of earth and fire. It is important, especially for beginners, to retain the basic integrity of the medium.

WHERE DOES IT COME FROM?

Clay comes from the earth. In the simplest terms, it is formed by the decomposition of rocks. It is the end product of rocks' weathering. Since geological erosion is an ongoing process, clay is a common and abundant material continually being formed by nature as the earth's crust disintegrates.

Clay is produced primarily by the weathering of granite and other feldspathic rock. Feldspar is composed of three basic elements—silicon, aluminum, and flux. These are the essential ingredients of clay, making up about 75 percent to 80 percent of the bulk of most clays.

TYPES OF CLAYS

Geologically, clays are divided into two categories— primary (or residual) and secondary (or sedimentary) clays. Primary clays are those that still remain in "pockets" in the areas in which they were formed; that is, clays that have not moved from their original site. Since the clay has not been worked over by the elements, it is often coarse-grained and relatively nonplastic. And, since it has not come into contact with other materials, it is usually quite pure. Primary clays are formed by the action of ground water on almost pure feldspar rock. These deposits are unusual, since small particles of weathered rock are normally carried away by rivers and streams and are eventually transported to other locations.

Secondary clays are those that do not remain in the areas in which they were formed. They have been transported away from their original site by the forces of nature, primarily through the work of water (rain, rivers, glaciers), wind, and natural erosion. These clays tend to be less pure, finer grained, and more plastic than primary clays. They are the clays most often used in making pottery in a studio workshop.

Within these two broad geological categories, there are many kinds of clay. In their natural state, it is unlikely that you will find many clay deposits yielding exactly the same types of clay. Clay varies greatly in color, purity, texture, plasticity, and porosity.

Clay in its natural state is difficult to work with. While digging and preparing your own clay may be an adventure worth experiencing (see Chapter 3), it is of course easier and, in general, more advisable to buy clay commercially. Here you know that the clay is of uniform consistency and fairly free of impurities and that it has been tested for such variables as plasticity and firing range. You can buy the type that is most suitable for the projects you have in mind as well as appropriate for the heat level and glazes you wish to use.

NATURAL CLAY VERSUS CLAY BODIES

In discussions of ceramics, you will often hear the terms natural clays and clay bodies. These terms may seem somewhat confusing at first, but they are really quite easy to explain. Very simply a natural clay is a clay (with such foreign materials as rocks, twigs, grasses, and dirt removed) that has not been altered in composition since it was dug from the ground. Some varieties are kaolin, a high-fire white clay used in making porcelain; ball clay, a clay added to kaolin to make it more plastic; and stoneware clay, a smooth plastic clay capable of withstanding high temperatures. There are other varieties such as earthenware clay, fire clay, and bentonite. These are natural clays. Sometimes they can be used successfully just as they come from the earth. More often, they are combined with each other and with some other materials such as sand or grog—clay that has been bisqued (fired only once) and ground—to form clay bodies. Clay bodies are mixtures of natural clays and other ceramic material that are blended to make a more predictable and easier-to-work-with product. The ceramic clays available commercially are clay bodies rather than natural clays.

SOME CLAY BODIES

Porcelain

Porcelain is the highest-firing clay body used in ceramic ware. It is often used in commercial pottery. Because of the extreme temperatures required for its maturation (2,300° F. to 2,800° F.), it is generally not used in most home or studio kilns. It is possible to fire porcelain successfully at lower temperatures, especially if the pieces made are decorative in nature rather than functional. Since porcelain vitrifies (becomes glasslike) at temperatures above 2,300° F., objects fired at lower temperatures may be porous. Porcelain at its usual range matures to a hard, white, translucent finish.

The two most common ceramic clay bodies with which you will be working in hand-crafted pottery are earthenware and stoneware bodies.

Earthenware

Much hand-crafted pottery is made from earthenware bodies. These are low-firing clays suitable for use in hand-building and wheel work. They are often red in color due to their heavy iron content. However, earthenware clays may also be white, gray, or light brown. They are highly plastic and easy to work with. Pottery made from earthenware clay must be glazed to be watertight, but even then it sometimes has a tendency to "sweat." (This means that enough water may escape through a glazed form to leave a watermark on a wooden table.)

Stoneware

Stoneware clays withstand higher heat than earthenware clays. They are plastic high-fire clays, with both the plasticity and firing range varying according to the composition of the particular clay. They are especially useful for making pottery since they often are adaptable to a wide variety of glazes. They are more suitable for containers that hold water than are earthenware clays, since their high firing temperatures should render them nonporous even when unglazed. Stoneware glazed and fired to maturation is completely watertight.

There are two ways to get clay for your pottery projects. You can buy the clay at a shop that sells ceramic supplies or you can dig your own. Both have their advantages and disadvantages.

DIGGING YOUR OWN CLAY

If you live in or are traveling through an area where there is a natural clay deposit, digging your own clay can be quite an adventure. Sometime in your wanderings you may come upon a deposit unexpectedly, perhaps near the banks of a river or lake. Because there are so many prepared clays available that give excellent (and predictable) results, you will probably want to rely mainly on these as your basic source of supply. However, digging as a sometime experience can be a great deal of fun and provide you with many new insights into clay. If nothing else, it will help you appreciate the convenience of the store-bought variety.

There is more involved in digging your own clay than a shovel and a strong arm. First you must find a clay deposit. Then you must recognize just which part of the "dirt" is clay. The clay will have a different feel from the surrounding earth. In its wet state, it will look smoother, shinier, and feel stickier than "plain dirt." As it dries it will hold together in masses or balls. The particles will be smaller than the surrounding soil, more like dust than sand. It is most likely to dry in clumps. These, when dropped, will shatter and appear powdery. So when you are searching for clay, look for smooth, sticky, "plastic" mud. Sometimes the clay will be gray in color, sometimes red, reddish brown, beige, or almost any earth color. The colors and texture will vary, depending on the locale and the mineral composition of the clay.

Finding the clay is only the first step. Then the clay must be dug, transported to your workshop, and cleaned. While the clay you dig is free, it extracts its cost in time spent. But it is time well spent if the experience gives you enjoyment and adds to your knowledge of the medium. Here are the steps in digging your own clay:

Step 1: Get one or more pails or other large containers and dig up as much wet clay as you think you will need.

Step 2: Take the clay home and let it dry thoroughly. This often takes several days. You can speed up the process by spreading the clay in a thin layer on a flat surface.

Step 3: Spread the dry clay on a large table or board and pound it with a rolling pin, baseball bat, or heavy stick, until it becomes very fine, like small grains of sand or dirt. As an alternative, grind it in an old coffee- or meat-grinder.

Step 4: Sift this through a large kitchen strainer or window screen to get out all lumps and foreign materials such as sticks, pebbles, and dried grass. Now you have clay powder. If the powder is not fine enough, sift it through a screen with smaller openings.

Step 5: The clay powder may now be stored for future use or, by adding water, converted into usable moist clay. To do this, put some water in a large container. Use a lot of water for a lot of clay, a little water for a little clay. Now slowly slake or sift in about one-half to three-quarters as much clay powder as you have water. Allow the clay to absorb the water before stirring. This will help you avoid a lumpy mixture. Stir until the clay is moistened. Keep stirring for a few minutes, mixing the powder thoroughly with the water.

Step 6: Let this mixture stand about half a day. The clay, because of its density, will sink to the bottom of the container while the water rises to the top. Now it is easy to pour off the excess water. The clay will still be very wet, so put it on an unvarnished board or plaster surface until it is dry enough to be kneaded. If the clay does not seem malleable enough, a little bentonite or ball clay may be added to improve plasticity. If it is too plastic, a little flint may be added. These materials are available at ceramic supply stores.

Step 7: Store any clay you will not be using in a plastic bag. Put it in a covered container in a place where it will retain moisture. Allow the clay to age for about three weeks before using it. This is necessary to make the clay easily workable.

Now that you have dug, cleaned, and prepared your own clay your insights into this material are much more intense. You have seen it at its original site, separated it from the surrounding materials, handled it in its various stages—from very wet to very dry—felt it, smelled it, pounded it, and strained it. You have been present at all its stages from a clump of dried mud full of sticks and stones to the finished, workable, plastic material. You have invested time and effort in your dealings with this mud, but you also have the pride of taking the first step in making a "silk purse out of a sow's ear," an opportunity that does not present itself every day. But, even after all these steps, your work is not quite completed. You must now test the clay for such variables as workability (how well can you manipulate it? how do the damp forms hold up?), changes while drying (how much does the clay shrink while drying? does it warp?), and maturation (is it a low- or high-fire clay? Chances are that it will be in the earthenware, or low-firing, range). You may find that, after testing, you will want to add some "store-bought" clay to your "home-dug" variety to make up a clay body of your own. With some luck and a little experimentation, you may create a clay body that works very well for you.

BUYING CLAY

Buying your clay from a store that handles pottery supplies is the easiest and surest way of getting the clay that is most suitable for the projects you wish to undertake. Clay is not an expensive material. It can be obtained at ceramic supply houses as well as some craft and hobby shops. It comes in large or small quantities and can be purchased moist and ready to use or as dry powder to which water must be added. It is packaged in quantities as small as five pounds or as large as fifty pounds. The more clay you buy, the cheaper the cost per pound. Initially it is best to purchase clay in small amounts—five-pound bags for sample experiments, or no more than twenty-five pounds at a time for larger endeavors. This way you can try several different types to see which one is most suitable for the pottery you will be making. A twenty-five-pound bag, enough for making twelve to twenty-four small to medium pieces, will cost about $3.50 a bag—perhaps slightly more if purchased moist, slightly less if ordered in dry form. Prices in clay, as in all other products, vary greatly from store to store and area to area.

The advantages of buying clay from a reputable dealer include the following: (1) you are able to buy the clay best suited to your specific needs; (2) you can buy as much or as little as you want; (3) you can buy it in dry or wet form; (4) the clay you buy has already been tested for such attributes as plasticity, porosity, and firing temperatures; and (5) the moist clay has been de-aired (an advantage when preparing the clay for work). This clay is predictable and will generally perform much the same way when fired at the same temperature. When you buy a white earthenware clay or a brown stoneware clay, you can then pick the proper glazes for these clay bodies and predict with fair accuracy what the finished product will look like. Fair accuracy are the key words here (especially for the beginner) because the interaction of clay, glaze, and heat are never totally predictable, a fact that accounts for some of the nicest surprises as well as the biggest disappointments in the craft of pottery.

How to Buy—Wet or Dry?

Clay may be bought either in its wet or dry form. Both have advantages. The main advantage of buying clay in its moist form is that it is ready to use as soon as it comes out of the bag. It has been de-aired, so wedging (clay preparation) takes less time. It has the right consistency and is uniform throughout. This is of special importance to the beginner. Since he has little or no experience in working with clay, he often does not know to what consistency to mix dry clay. After handling moist purchased clay of suitable plasticity, he can later mix dry clay to approximate this consistency. This is the primary reason moist clay is recommended for initial experiences. This clay is conveniently packaged in plastic storage bags.

The advantages of buying clay in dry form are that it is somewhat less expensive than prepared clay and is easier to store. You can mix as little or as much as you want. (However, the clay should be aged for several weeks to improve plasticity, so, unlike moist clay, it is not suitable for immediate use.) It can be used for mixing with other clay bodies and materials to make up clay bodies of your own.

Clay may also be purchased in a liquid form called slip. This is used in plaster casting, making clay objects with the use of a plaster mold. The casting body may be bought in powdered form and mixed with water. As with other clays, the dry form is somewhat less expensive and easier to store than the product ready for instant use.

Some Things to Consider When Buying Clay

It is important to buy the right clay for the right purpose. One of the main factors to consider is what temperatures the kiln you will use for firing the finished ware attains. Different clay bodies fire at different temperatures. It is necessary to use a clay within the range of the kiln at your disposal. It would generally make little sense to try to fire a porcelain clay body that needs extreme heat in a low-fire electric kiln, since the porcelain would not mature under these conditions. Conversely, it would be disastrous to fire a low-firing earthenware pot at temperatures suited for high-fire stoneware, since the earthenware would deform or melt at these high temperatures. So know the firing range of your kiln, and buy clays and glazes that are suited to its temperatures.

Firing temperature is only one of the considerations in choosing your clay. Different methods of working with clay will lead you to choose clays most appropriate for that particular method. For instance, clay that is best for modeling will not necessarily be best for wheel work. Sculpting clay would be totally unsuitable for casting. To find out initially which of the many available clay bodies will give the best results with different techniques, ask. The personnel at the ceramic supply shop where you buy the clay will be able to answer most of your questions and to suggest several clays well suited for your purpose. Larger ceramic supply houses will often send you, on request, a catalogue that describes clays, glazes, and other supplies in detail, providing an excellent guide for purchasing pottery materials. As you continue to experiment in this area, you will develop your own preferences.

The essential ingredient for making pottery is clay. With the exception of a potter's wheel and kiln—purchases not recommended until you feel a real commitment to the craft—the materials you will need are relatively few and low in cost. Some can be found in your own home, and the rest can be readily purchased at a hardware store, hobby shop, or of course the dealer from whom you buy your clay.

If you are interested in using a potter's wheel (one of the most exciting ways of creating clay pieces), enroll in a course at a recreation center, an adult school, your local college, or a private studio, where basic instruction and the use of the wheel are provided. Your homemade pieces may be fired at ceramic shops that provide such facilities. Often there is little or no charge for firing if the glazes are purchased there. Otherwise there will be a reasonable firing fee, usually depending upon how much space your pots take up in the kiln. If you are taking a pottery class, firing will be provided. There may be a small glaze fee for each piece fired, depending on the size of the piece and the amount of glaze used.

The best "tools" to use in making pottery are your own hands and fingers. A "handmade" pot should be just that. The less interference there is from other "tools," the more essentially "handcrafted" your piece will be. Especially in the beginning you will want as much "communication" with the clay as possible to really get the feel of the material. However it is not necessary to be a total purist. There are a few tools that can give your pottery a more finished look and greatly facilitate the process of working with clay. Here is a list of some of the basic tools that should comprise your pottery kit.

4

BEFORE YOU BEGIN

MATERIALS

Besides the clay, a container in which to store it, and water to use while you work on it, you will need the following:

1. A container for water.

2. A container for carrying and storing your tools. An empty metal coffee can or a plastic bleach bottle with the top cut off works quite well.

3. A fairly large piece of oilcloth to cover your work surface.

4. A small elephant ear sponge. This is a special fine-grained sponge sold in ceramic supply houses.

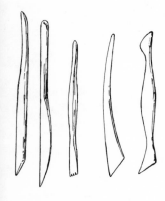

5. At least one wooden modeling tool.

6. Several plaster bats. These are useful both for hand-building and wheel work. They can easily be made at home by pouring plaster of Paris mixed with water into oiled pie pans of varying sizes. To mix plaster, always sift the plaster into the water—do not pour the water into the plaster. Mix to the consistency of thick cream. As the plaster hardens, it will shrink slightly. The oil will help it slide easily from the pan. (Never, never, never, pour excess plaster down your drain or toilet bowl. This can cause plumbing problems of gigantic proportions. Pour extra plaster in a disposable container and deposit it in your garbage can.)

7. A cutting wire. This is a thin wire with wooden handles at each end. It is used for cutting clay.

8. A needle for testing clay thickness. This tool may be bought commercially or may be made by inserting a long needle into a large cork.

9. A fettling knife (knife with a long flexible narrow blade).

10. A wooden and/or metal rib and/or rubber kidney. These are useful for refining pieces, for example, eliminating finger marks from the inside of a bowl. They may be purchased at ceramic supply houses.

11. At least one wire loop or trimming tool. Though there are several varieties available especially for trimming pottery, a pear pitter, which can be bought in many shops carrying kitchen supplies, will work just as well.

12. Several good brushes for glazing. This is one area where it pays to spend a little more money for a better product. Cheap brushes often do not do a satisfactory job of holding and applying glaze and will tend to wear out far sooner than brushes of good quality. Buy at least one small-, medium-, and large-tipped brush. You may want some pointed ones and some flat ones. A flat brush about 1-inch wide is most often used when applying a coat of glaze to a whole pot. Smaller brushes are generally used for designing.

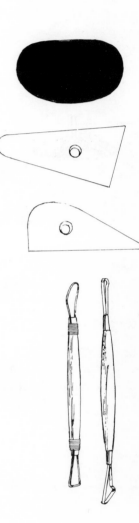

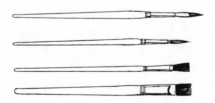

13. Glazes are fairly expensive. Initially buy a few commercially prepared glazes in small amounts (often you can buy as little as four ounces). Be sure to buy glazes suitable for your clay body and within the firing range of the kiln you will be using. Often the supply house where you buy the glazes will

have samples of what the glaze will look like on certain types of clay bodies fired at a specific temperature. Although these can guide you in making a decision, do not expect your pottery to turn out exactly like these glaze samples.

14. A banding wheel or turntable is not a necessary accoutrement, but it is nice to have when making round forms. It is a small wheel on a turntable and is available at ceramic supply houses. When you are working on a round form (or in glazing), the banding wheel may be rotated, enabling you to work freely on all sides of the pot without constant handling of the pot itself. A Lazy Susan with a flat base will also work.

These tools are useful in many areas of pottery. Others needed for specific techniques will be listed at the beginning of each project.

PREPARING THE CLAY

Now that you have gotten your clay and assembled your tools, it is time to prepare the clay for work.

Mixing Dry Clay

If you have purchased your clay in dry form, it must first be made into moist clay before it can be worked. The procedure for mixing powdered clay that you dig yourself may be followed, or you can mix according to the following directions.

Step 1: Pour some water into a large bowl or other good-sized container.

Step 2: Slowly sift or slake clay powder into the water, a little at a time, allowing the water to absorb the dry clay. Continue adding more clay powder until the mixture is quite thick.

Step 3: Let the clay stand for about half an hour to be sure that all particles are thoroughly saturated.

Step 4: Now stir the mixture with a large wooden spoon or paddle until it is even in consistency and free of lumps. (If you begin to stir while adding the clay, you will have a lumpy mixture, since the clay will not have had time to absorb sufficient water.)

Step 5: Spread the wet clay on a plaster bat and allow it to dry until it can be worked.

Step 6: Form it into several balls and allow it to age for a few weeks (about three weeks or more is a proper amount of time). Wedge as needed for use.

Another alternative is to mix the dry clay right in the plastic bag in which it is packaged. To each pound of clay add four to five ounces of water. Squeeze the air out of the bag and tie the bag opening securely with string. Now knead the clay right in the bag until the clay and water are thoroughly mixed. This is a convenient way of mixing dry clay, since it requires no utensils and eliminates clean-up chores. Allow the clay to age several weeks to improve plasticity. Wedge.

WEDGING

It is not advisable to begin working with clay, premixed or not, just as it comes from the bag. Some initial preparation is needed. The clay may be uneven in texture or it may contain air bubbles—conditions that will lead to unsatisfactory results in your finished product. Air bubbles may ruin an otherwise well-crafted piece by causing it to crack or break in the process of drying or firing. They are also especially annoying when you are working on the potter's wheel, as they will cause your fingers to "trip" on the walls of the pot, creating lumps, bumps, and uneven walls and often causing the pot to collapse altogether. Many potentially well-thrown pots have been ruined because of air bubbles left in by inadequate wedging. Wedging is a process used to remove air bubbles from the clay, by forcing them out, and to make the clay uniform in texture.

Although wedging tables are usually made from plaster, unfinished wood works almost as well, since its surface too absorbs moisture and the clay does not stick to it. A sheet of unfinished plywood makes an excellent wedging surface. A large kitchen cutting board may also be used successfully for wedging.

There are several ways to wedge.

Method I

One effective method of wedging is to "knead" the clay. Although this process may seem familiar to those who are adept at making bread, its goal is actually the opposite. In bread-making, it is desirable to knead as much air as possible into the dough. In wedging clay, the aim is to force out excess air.

Step 1: Form the clay into a ball.

Step 2: With one hand on each side of the mass, bring the clay toward you, pressing down on the wedging board with the balls of your hands as you knead. Contain the clay with your hands and move

it toward you, so that the outside of the clay comes toward the center. Press down, pushing the air bubbles out, then lift clay toward you on the board. Continue this procedure until you think the clay is wedged. (A little practice will help you make an educated guess.)

Step 3: Slice the clay in half with your cutting wire. Check for air bubbles. These appear as tiny holes on the cut surface of the clay. Slice clay three or four times to check for bubbles. If the clay

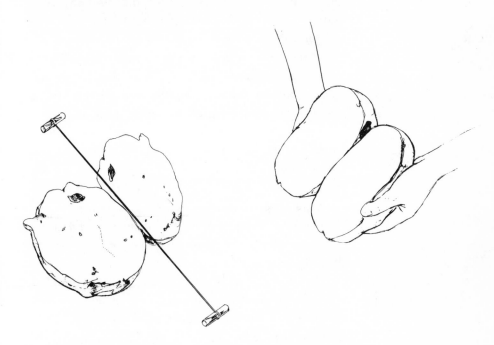

is smooth and even, wedging is completed and the clay is ready to be formed. If air bubbles are present, continue wedging the clay as before, kneading as described fifteen or twenty times more.

Step 4: After you have repeated the wedging process again, slice the clay with a cutting wire. If no small holes appear, the clay may now be used for any method of pottery making.

Method II

Another method of wedging is to remove air bubbles by throwing the clay down hard on a solid surface. While this method is often used, it is not, in the opinion of this author, as effective as Method I.

Step 1: Form the clay into a ball.

Step 2: Throw the clay ball down hard on a cutting board, sheet of plywood, or plaster wedging table. If none of these is available, use any solid surface such as your kitchen table covered with oilcloth. (Turn oilcloth shiny side down.) Repeat this throwing-down process ten to twenty times. Try to slap the clay down in such a way that all its surfaces come in contact with the wedging area. This forces air bubbles out of the whole mass of clay.

Step 3: Now cut the clay in half with your cutting wire and check for air bubbles. Slap the cut surfaces down on your wedging board, one on top of the other. Slice clay again to check for bubbles. If none appear, further wedging is not required. If air bubbles are present, continue wedging by slapping down the mass of clay another ten to twenty times.

Step 4: Again slice your clay to check for bubbles. The clay is ready for use when it is of uniform consistency and free of air bubbles.

There are other methods of wedging similar to the two described here. It does not matter which you choose as long as the result is a clay of even consistency and free of air bubbles.

Note: After you become proficient in wedging and are able to assess accurately that your clay is well wedged, it is no longer necessary to slice it to check for air bubbles—as cutting and rejoining may cause air pockets to form.

RECONDITIONING THE CLAY

As long as the clay has not been fired, it can be reworked and used again. Even if the piece has already dried, the clay can be broken up and, with the addition of water, made reusable for future projects.

Save all your clay scraps. If they are still wet enough, they can be rewedged immediately to make another pot. If the clay has dried out, it can be stored in a container to which water may be added at any time. Collect all your dry "trimmings." Put them in a pail. Add a sufficient amount of water to cover, and let the clay "sit" in this for a day or two. Pour off the excess water and spread the clay on a plaster bat to dry. When it has dried to workable consistency, rewedge and use again.

STORING

Clay powder can be stored in any suitable container and mixed as the situation warrants, by adding powder to water or by mixing in the heavy plastic bag.

Moist clay should be stored in a heavy plastic bag and, if possible, be placed in a lidded container. If the clay is kept from drying out, allowing it to age for a few weeks will increase its workability.

If the clay is too wet after storage, it can be dried on a plaster bat until it reaches the proper consistency. If it is too dry, place a damp towel in the plastic bag, reclose the bag, and keep the towel inside for two or three days. This process will effectively soften the clay with no further effort on your part. If it is necessary to use the clay immediately, poke a few holes into it and add a bit of water. Work the water in with your hands. If you have time, the former method is easier and often more successful than the latter.

GROG

Grog is clay that has been fired once and then ground up into particles. It is often used to decrease the shrinkage of fine clay. You may want to add grog to your clay for reasons that are both functional and artistic. Functionally, grog makes clay more porous. It is useful in making tiles or other flat pieces since it reduces the shrinkage of the clay and, therefore, also the possibility of warping (sometimes a problem with projects of this nature). It is often added in fairly large amounts to clay that will be used for sculpture or large hand-built forms (especially those made by the slab technique), since it gives the clay more body and makes it "hold up" better. It is not advisable to add large portions of grog to clay that will be used to make vases, cups, and other vessels. Because it increases the clay's porosity, grog is best used in pieces that do not have to be completely watertight.

Grog may be added to clay used either for hand-building or for wheel work. However, if it is used in clay that will be thrown, it is important that the grog be fine. Otherwise the clay will be too abrasive and can cut your hands as they press down on the revolving material.

Grog is also used for aesthetic reasons, primarily as a texturing device. Grogged clay provides a rough sandy texture as contrasted with the smooth satiny texture of glazed ungrogged clay. When these two clays are used together, the textural variations add to the design qualities of the piece. Grog is generally incorporated into the clay before the piece is formed, often during the wedging process. As a texturing technique, it may also be patted onto a finished moist piece.

DRYING

After the clay has been formed it should be allowed to dry slowly. It is best to make your creation as uniform in thickness as possible and not over an inch thick in any part. While a form may be modeled "solid," it should be hollowed out when (or before) it reaches the "leather-hard" stage. Drying time depends on the size of the piece. Small thin pieces dry quickly. Large heavy ones take much longer.

If the clay is not uniform in thickness, the thinner parts will dry faster than the thicker ones. Unless the piece is covered with plastic or a damp cloth (or both), it will dry unevenly and crack or warp. It may be necessary to sponge some surfaces (like the rim of a bowl) with a little water to keep them from drying faster than the rest of the piece. Air should also be allowed to circulate around the

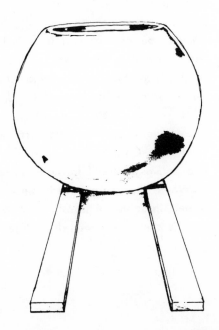

bottom of the pot so this area will dry at a rate similar to the rest of the piece. One way of ensuring this is to support your pot on two even strips of wood. This will enable the air to get under it as well as around it.

If you are working on a piece that cannot be completed in one sitting, the ideal place to store it is a damp box—a cupboard with tight-fitting doors containing plaster shelves that are periodically wetted down with water to keep the clay pieces stored there from drying out. Since a damp box is generally not available except in a well-equipped studio, there are other ways of keeping a pot from drying past the leather-hard stage for a few days. It is possible to make a simple "damp" storage box from a large corrugated paper box lined with tin foil or plastic sheeting. If your piece is placed on a damp bat and the box is inverted over it, it should retain sufficient moisture for several days. It is a good idea to wet down the bat each day by sprinkling a few drops of water on it.

A plastic bag from a dry cleaner or supermarket or even a small sandwich bag (depending upon the size of the piece) will also retard drying. Often this is all that will be needed.

Clay goes through several stages while drying. When you are shaping it, it is in its plastic state. As it dries it becomes leather-hard. This means that it is too hard to manipulate but still soft enough to be trimmed, carved, textured, or added on to. This is a good stage at which to join pieces that have several parts or add such features as handles or knobs. Care must be taken to deal gently with the pot, as it is still fairly sensitive to pressure.

When the leather-hard piece loses even more water through evaporation, it becomes bone-dry. This is the completely dry stage at which the pot must arrive before it can be fired. Do not try to fire a pot that is still "just a little wet." If it is not completely dry, the intense heat of the kiln will almost surely cause it to crack or even explode. In addition to losing this one pot, you may damage many other pieces in the kiln. If the piece has been exposed to air at room temperature for at least a week, you can be reasonably sure that it is ready to fire. Of course drying time varies greatly, depending on such factors as the thickness of the piece and the humidity of the air.

Clay shrinks about 5 to 8 percent while drying and again, the same amount, or even a bit more, in firing. Therefore, the fired piece will be about 15 percent smaller than the original creation.

FIRING AND GLAZING

After the clay has been thoroughly dried, it is fired in a kiln—a furnace that reaches very high temperatures (about 1,800° to 2,000° F. for earthenware and higher for stoneware and porcelain). This process changes the piece from a fragile, reusable mass of clay into a hard, durable, permanent form.

Clay that has not been fired is called greenware. Clay that has been fired once is called bisque ware. After the bisque-firing, the piece may be left unglazed—for flower pots, beads, tiles, sculpture, and various decorative pieces—or it may be glazed and fired again. The glaze-firing again changes the character of the piece. When a pot is bisque-fired, it is still porous and does not make a suitable container for holding foods or liquids. Once a pot has been glaze-fired, the glass coating generally makes the pot watertight. Although glazes are used for their decorative value, they have a functional one as well.

5

GETTING THE "FEEL" OF THINGS

The clay is wedged, the tools are assembled, and you are raring to go. Before learning specific techniques of working with clay, it is important to get the "feel" of the medium, to see what it will and won't do.

A kitchen table makes a fine work surface. Cover it with a piece of oilcloth, placed slick side down. The rough texture of the underside will keep the clay from sticking to the cloth. Always have an elephant ear sponge and a container of water at your side as you work.

EXERCISES IN MANIPULATION

Begin by rolling small pieces of clay into balls. Observe how smooth the clay feels in your hands. Notice that the heat of your skin has a drying effect on the clay. You will also see that if the clay is worked too long and becomes too dry it cracks. Smoothing a little water over it with a sponge will keep it properly moist.

Now take some of the balls and elongate them into tapered ovals or short coils. Roll them between your palms, changing their shape by the pressure of your hands. Flatten some into pancakes. Be aware at all times of what the touch of your hands does to the clay. Although this may seem like a waste of time, you are actually becoming familiar with the process of manipulation and the reaction of the clay to different types of pressure. This is the basis of most techniques in working with clay. The time spent in familiarizing yourself with the qualities of the medium is time well spent.

Roll some of the clay balls into long, thin coils. Roll others into short, fat coils. Flatten some of the coils by pressing them down on the table. Bend and twist others to see how much stress they can endure without breaking.

Using natural materials and materials found around the home to texture the surface of moist clay. (*Photograph by Howard M. Berliant*)

EXERCISES IN TEXTURE

Pat a piece of clay into a large smooth pancake. Lay the pancake down on the worktable and make indentations in it with your thumb and fingers. See what sort of pattern the pressure of your thumb makes on the clay. Use all surfaces of your fingers (such as tips and knuckles) to press designs into the clay. Scratch or gouge the surface with your fingernails. Note how the clay responds. Many pleasing textures can be created in this manner.

Flatten a ball of clay and then roll it out with a rolling pin. (A square about 12 inches by 12 inches or a little larger is a good size.) Using simple objects that you have around the house, vary its

Texture imprinted on moist clay. Detail from a vase by Michi Zimmerman. (*Photograph By Howard M. Berliant*)

texture by pressing designs into it. Use the bowl of a spoon, the tines of a fork (making both straight and wavy lines), the teeth of a comb, or nail and screw heads. Press paper clips, buttons, dry sponge, or string into it. If you have pieces of rough bark, seashells, nuts, beans, textured rocks, or fossils, use them to print designs. The variety of textures that can be obtained by a quick forage in your kitchen cabinets is great enough to keep you busy for one or two work sessions. Experimentation at this stage will give you many pleasant possibilities to use when it becomes time to texture finished pots. It will also help you avoid some fiascos. Later you may want to make some decorative clay or plaster stamps for imprinting specific designs.

Roll, pinch, squeeze, pound, texture, cut—in other words, "play" with the clay. If possible, use several different kinds of clay and see if the same process varies, depending upon the type of clay used. Wedge a little grog into some of the clay. See how this changes the look and feel of the composition. Pat grog over parts of a smooth clay ball, coil, or pancake. See what effects this has on the appearance. Notice the contrast in textures.

When you are satisfied that you have gotten the basic feel of the clay, it is time to proceed to the specific projects and techniques of building described in the following chapters.

Large stoneware assembled pot. Combed surface. Artist Richard Fairbanks. Antonio Prieto Collection of Modern Ceramics, Mills College. (Photograph by Margaret d'Hamer)

For all projects in this book, you will need a work surface, wedged clay, an elephant ear sponge, water, plus various tools from your pottery kit. Materials other than these will be listed at the beginning of each project.

Instructions given will include steps up to the first firing. Decorating and glazing techniques and firing procedures are discussed in separate chapters.

Since many of these clay experiences "build" upon each other, it is recommended that these projects be done in order whenever possible or at least that general directions for a specific technique be read before undertaking creations in this area.

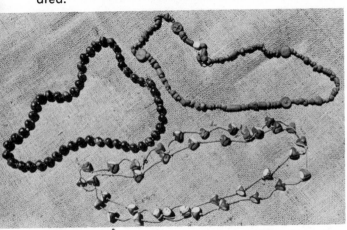

Various types of beads. Round raku beads (left) by Joanne Somerville. Unglazed beads, some painted with engobes (right) by Bruce Beasley. Natural clay and glazed beads (center), student work. *(Photograph by Howard M. Berliant)*

6

SIMPLE CLAY PROJECTS

BEADS

MATERIALS
Long nail
Texturing tools or devices (optional)

A small ball of wedged clay will make quite a few beads. Beads do not have to be round. They can be oval, cylindrical, square, large or small, short or long, fairly flat, or three dimensional. When working with clay, keep in mind that the clay shrinks about 15 percent in total. So make both the bead *and* the hole larger than you want them to be when finished.

Step 1: Roll a small bit of clay into a ball. The bead may be left round or worked into any of the shapes mentioned above. Another way of making beads is to roll some clay into a coil of the desired width and slice the coil into beads of pleasing length.

Step 2: Beads may be left smooth, or designs may be pressed into them at this stage. You might flatten some out and press walnut shell halves or eucalyptus fruits into them. (Do not make them too thin.) Vary size, shape, texture, and over-all appearance.

Step 3: Allow the beads to dry until they are almost leather-hard. Poke a hole through the center of each bead with a long nail. Be sure that the hole is the same width on both sides of the bead. This can be accomplished by poking the nail through

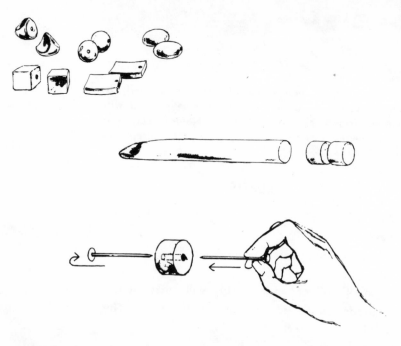

one end and then the other. Smooth any rough spots with a sponge.

Step 4: When the beads are leather-hard, they may be carved with a sharp tool or textured by using a knife or by pricking or scraping with fork tines, nails, and so on. (This step is optional.)

Step 5: Allow the beads to dry thoroughly before firing. Depending upon the color of clay, the amount of texturing, and the type of firing, you may want to leave the beads unglazed, to apply engobe (white or colored slip) to some, or to glaze some or all of them. For firing see specific directions for beads in Chapter 17.

Ceramic buttons, textured and plain. By the author and Anni Grundler. *(Photograph by Howard M. Berliant)*

BUTTONS

MATERIALS
Nail for poking holes

Buttons are made in much the same way as beads. Here again keep in mind that there are many variations on the more orthodox round form. Buttons as well as beads become more interesting when varied in size and shape. When making small objects, be especially aware of the shrinkage of the clay, and be sure to make both the object and the hole larger than the finished product needs to be. (A button that will not accommodate a needle through its holes is useless.)

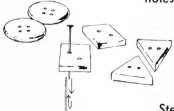

Step 1: Roll a small piece of clay between your palms as if you were making a bead. When the clay is round and smooth, flatten it into a tiny pancake. If you wish to vary the round form, mold the button into the shape of your choice with your fingers. Smooth any cracks with a damp sponge.

Step 2: Allow the button to dry on a flat surface until the button is almost leather-hard. (You may leave it on the work surface or bat where it was made.)

Step 3: With a nail, make two to four holes in the button so it can be sewn onto a garment.

Step 4: When the button is leather-hard, poke the nail through the holes from the back, to make sure that the hole is even front and back. Smooth any rough spots with a sponge.

Step 5: Allow your buttons to dry thoroughly before firing.

Note: For making buttons with a shank, complete the basic form. Do not make holes in it. Instead, roll a tiny coil, form this into a loop, and fasten it to the back of the button. Use a toothpick to attach and blend the loop onto the button back.

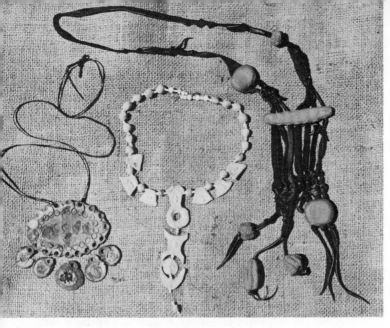

Ceramic necklaces. Raku pendant with attached pieces (left) by Joanne Somerville. Ceramic and seed bead necklace (center) by Andrée Thompson. Ceramic and leather necklace (right) by Anni Grundler. (Photograph by Howard M. Berliant)

JEWELRY

Pendants, Pins, and Earrings

MATERIALS
Paper and pencil
Cardboard
Scissors
Rolling pin
Sharp knife
Nail
Cookie-cutter (optional)
"Findings": pin backs, earring backs or wires, pendant link, chain, or other hanging device for pendant
White glue or liquid cement

Pendants, earrings, and pins can be made according to the same general directions as beads and buttons.

Step 1: Experiment on paper with shapes that you find pleasing.

Step 2: Transfer the shape you choose to use for your design onto cardboard. Cut this out with scissors. It is your pattern.

Step 3: Take a small ball of wedged clay, flatten it out on your work surface, and roll it with a rolling pin to about ⅛ to ¹/₁₆ of an inch thickness. Occasionally, pendants and pins may be somewhat thicker, particularly if they are also large.

Step 4: Place the pattern on the clay and cut around it with a sharp knife. Allow the piece to dry on the work surface until it is almost leather-hard.

Step 5: An alternative to making paper patterns is to use a cookie-cutter as a pattern. While this is neither suitable nor desirable for all your jewelry, a cookie-cutter Christmas tree or holly wreath might make an easy-to-do, effective holiday brooch or pendant. Cookie-cutter patterns can form the basis of some interesting personal variations as well.

Step 6: When the piece is almost leather-hard, smooth the edges and back with a sponge. For a pendant make a hole very close to the top so that a link may be inserted and the piece hung from a chain. For dangling earrings (either pierced or non-pierced), also make a hole at the top so that the proper findings may be inserted. "Findings" is the collective name for links, earring backs, clasps, and other objects used in making jewelry. They are available at most ceramic supply houses as well as many hobby and variety stores. As with beads and buttons, be sure to poke the nail through the hole from the back of the piece as well as the front.

Step 7: Allow the pieces to dry thoroughly. Smooth any rough area with fine sandpaper if necessary.

Step 8: After the piece has been fired, it may be decorated in your choice of techniques. Engobe decoration often looks very effective on large pend-

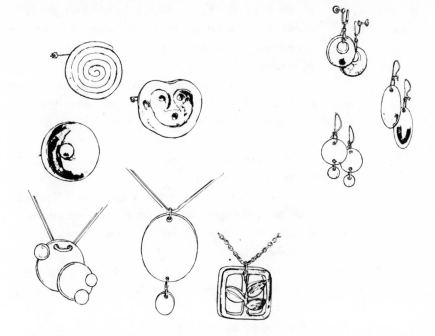

ants or pins (see chapter on glazing). When the piece is completed, findings are attached through its holes. Attach pin backs.

Ceramic pendants may be hung from chains but also look very effective suspended from leather thongs, macramé cord, or some types of ribbon.

Necklaces

The pieces described above were fashioned by making a form from one piece of clay and using that shape alone as the decorative piece of jewelry. It is also possible to join several shapes or sections to yield a more complex piece. When you create a necklace from a number of sections, the pieces may all be of the same size, shape, texture, and glaze treatment, or each section may vary in any or all of these areas. Since jewelry need serve no functional purpose, it is an ideal area in which to experiment with the solely decorative possibilities of ceramics.

The steps used in making multiple-section jewelry are basically the same as for single-form pieces. The design composition becomes more complex, however, since the choice of possible shapes for one necklace is of course extended from the single shape of a pendant.

Step 1: Draw your necklace on paper. You may wish to make the entire piece from flat slabs or to vary the design by incorporating beads as part of the necklace.

Step 2: Make a pattern for each piece. Place pattern pieces on properly rolled-out clay and cut around them with a sharp knife. Make beads if these are to be included.

Step 3: Allow the pieces to dry until they are almost leather-hard. With a sharp nail, poke holes into each section at the point where it will be attached to the chain, cord, or other object. Poke holes through beads as previously described. When making your holes, be sure they are large enough to accommodate the material you will be using to join the pieces.

Step 4: Allow all parts to dry thoroughly. Fire.

Step 5. After the pieces have been fired (and decorated and/or glazed, if you wish), join them to each other with metal links, nylon thread, leather strips, macramé twine, etc. Suspend the finished necklace from one of these materials or from a metal chain, cord, etc. Clasps may be attached to chain ends to facilitate opening and closing.

TILES

MATERIALS
Pencil
Cardboard
Scissors
Ruler
Two wooden strips or dowels (guide sticks) 12- to
    24-inches long and about ½- to 1-inch thick
Rolling pin
Sharp knife
Texturing devices (if desired)
Plastic bags or sheeting

Tiles have a tendency to warp. Any very flat piece, especially if large, may "curl" at the edges, since the outside normally begins to dry before the center. One way to decrease the amount of warping in a tile is to add heavy amounts of grog to

Textured tiles used as decorative forms over a fireplace. Michi Zimmerman. *(Photograph by Michi Zimmerman)*

the clay. You may add grog so that it makes up as much as 20 percent of the final amount of clay to be used or to put it another way, use one part grog to four parts clay. If you want to minimize its textural effects, use very fine grog; to emphasize them, use coarser grog. To add grog to clay, flatten the clay by hand or with a rolling pin. Sprinkle grog over its surface. Roll up as for a jelly roll. Knead the clay to mix the grog into it evenly. Wedge thoroughly.

It is not absolutely necessary to use grog. There are other ways to keep a tile from warping (see Step 7).

Step 1: Using a ruler, measure a square 6 inches by 6 inches and draw it on a piece of cardboard. Cut it out with a scissors. This will be the pattern for your tiles. Of course tiles may be made larger or smaller, but this is a good size for a first attempt. The thickness of the tile will depend upon its size. Small tiles will be thinner than large ones. In all areas of clay work, thickness should be kept in proportion to size.

Step 2: Take a large ball of wedged grogged clay and flatten it with your hands.

Step 3: Place two wooden guide strips ½- to 1-inch thick parallel to each other on your work surface. Place these sufficiently apart to accommodate the width of clay necessary for the project. Here, the sticks should be placed 6 to 12 inches apart—to make one or two tiles per width.

Step 4: Rest a rolling pin on the wooden strips and roll the clay evenly, pressing down gently. The strips serve as a guide to keep the rolled-out clay uniformly thick. Move the rolling pin up from the center and down from the center. If the rolling pin sticks to the clay, dust it with a little dry clay.

Step 5: When the clay has been rolled to uniform thickness place the pattern on it, and with a sharp knife carefully cut out the number of tiles you wish

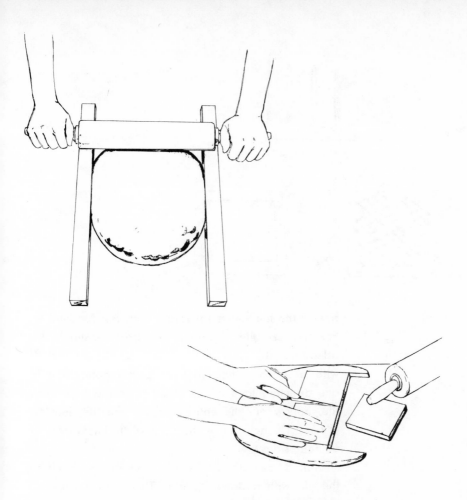

to make. Two to six is a good number for your first project.

Step 6: The tiles may be left smooth or they can be textured. You may want to use some of the texturing devices you evolved in your experimentation in textures (see page 41). Any sort of printing should be undertaken while the tile is still moist.

Step 7: There are several procedures that can be undertaken at this point to keep warping to a minimum. One method (rather than all) will suffice. (a) When the tiles are firm enough to handle easily, turn them over and hollow out several grooves in the back, using a wire modeling tool or sharp knife. The number of grooves will vary with the

size of the tile—more for larger tiles, less for smaller. For this size tile, three or four grooves should be adequate. (b) You may "score" the tile—scratch it with a sharp cutting tool, or pencil point, first in one direction then in the other. (c) For a very thick tile, hollow out the entire body of the tile, leaving a 1- or 1½-inch rim of the original thickness around all four sides.

Step 8: Smooth any rough spots on the back of the tile with a damp sponge. Then turn it face up and smooth rough areas on surface and corners. If you have not previously decorated your tile, it may now be carved. This, of course, is optional.

Step 9: Allow the tile to dry slowly. To retard drying time, the tiles may be covered with a sheet of thin plastic. If the edges tend to dry faster than the middle, these may be sponged lightly a few times as the tile dries. Or strips of plastic may be placed around the edges of the tile only. This way, the tile will dry from the middle to the edges.

Step 10: After the tiles are thoroughly dry, smooth any rough edges. Fire and glaze as desired.

The directions given here produce square tiles. The procedures used above will work just as well for round, rectangular, or triangular, tiles.

TRIVETS

MATERIALS

Same as for tiles

Slip or slurry (clay mixed with water to form liquid clay)

Follow directions for making tiles through Step 6.

Step 1: After making your tile, model three or four feet (supports) for each tile. These may be square, round, conical, or cylindrical.

Step 2: Allow both the tiles and feet to dry to the leather-hard stage.

Step 3: Follow Steps 7 and 8 in making tiles.

Step 4: Score the tiles with a sharp pencil or tool in the area where the feet are to be attached. Score the feet at the point of attachment. To score, scratch heavily one way and then another with a sharp instrument.

Step 5: Mix some clay with water to form slip or slurry. Smear a little slip on the scoring of both feet and tile at the point of attachment. Press feet into tile. Smooth slip into any cracks. Blend these areas with your sponge.

Step 6: Allow the trivet to dry slowly. Cover loosely with a thin sheet of plastic. Sponge corners and junctures if necessary. When the trivet is almost dry, remove plastic and allow to air dry.

Step 7: When the trivet has dried completely, smooth rough edges, paying particular attention to the areas where the feet were attached.

Step 8: Fire and glaze as desired.

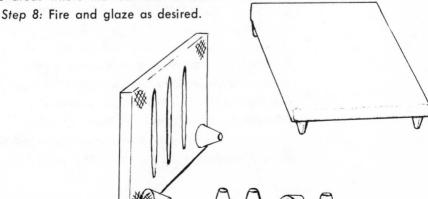

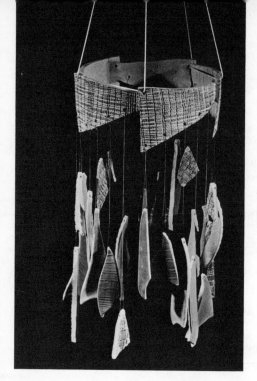

Mobile or wind chime. Unglazed oxide-stained clay made by Anni Grundler.
(Photograph by Howard M. Berliant)

HANGING PIECES—
MOBILES AND WIND CHIMES

MATERIALS
Pencil and paper
Cardboard
Rolling pin
Sharp knife
Two strips of wood about ⅜- to ½-inch thick and 24 inches long
Thin sheet of plastic
Slip
Leather strips, twine, wire, yarn, or fish line for hanging

Hanging pieces such as wind chimes or mobiles may be made by joining several pieces, using wire, fish line, and so on. Abstract or realistic shapes may be used for any of these creations.

Step 1: Experiment on paper until you have drawn some shapes that please you. Do not make anything elaborate at this time. Simple animal shapes (fish, birds, owls, cats) or abstract geometric designs lend themselves well to first experiences.

Step 2: Transfer the shapes to a piece of cardboard and cut them out for use as a pattern. You may suspend your mobile or wind chime from a clay base, or use a driftwood or wire base.

Step 3: Roll wedged clay between two guide sticks as in making tiles. When the clay has reached uniform thickness, place the pattern on it and cut around it with a sharp knife. For instant texture on one side of your pieces, roll out the clay on burlap or other roughly woven cloth. This will add interest to the side you may wish to leave unglazed or otherwise undecorated. Any designs to be printed on the clay should be undertaken now.

Step 4: Allow the pieces to dry almost to the leather-hard stage. Smooth any rough areas, both front and back, with a damp sponge.

Step 5: At this stage, the piece may be textured by carving or adding small pieces of clay to the basic form. Example—when making a fish or bird, the scales or feathers may be modeled from small balls of flattened clay attached with slip. Small pieces attached to the main body do not need scoring. Score for larger additions. Other bits of modeled clay may be put on for the eyes, beak, and wings for added texture. Details may also be incised with a sharp tool if you do not wish to add them on.

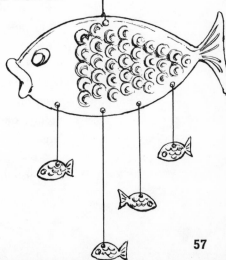

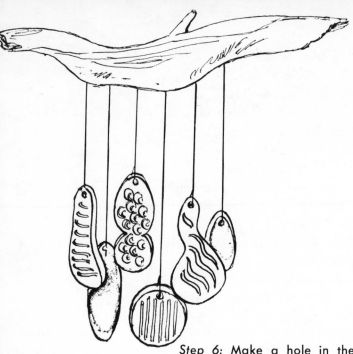

Step 6: Make a hole in the top of each piece so it may be hung. Push a nail through the front, then through the back, as in making jewelry. If you plan to attach hanging parts at the bottom of a piece, make a hole in the end as well. (Be sure to allow for shrinkage by making holes large enough.)

Step 7: If you have added parts to a main form, wipe away excess slip that may have oozed from points of attachment.

Step 8: Allow the pieces to dry slowly to the leather-hard stage. Cover with plastic sheeting to slow the drying process.

Step 9: Fire and glaze. Twine, leather strips, heavy yarn, or wire are suitable materials for hanging a main piece and may also be used for attaching one piece to another. Keep your "string" in harmony with the total finished design. You may want to use two different materials for hanging—for example, suspend the main piece from one or more leather thongs and attach smaller pieces with nylon fishing line.

Note: Cookie-cutters may also be used as patterns in creating pieces of this nature.

7

PINCH POTS

Pinch pots were probably the earliest kind of man-made clay pots. When our prehistoric ancestors first shaped wet clay into rude bowls, they molded it with their hands and fingers in much the same way we use for making pinch pots today. This technique has been in existence for thousands of years, and many beautiful and refined pieces may be made in this manner.

A pinch pot is a form made by "pinching" the clay—or squeezing it between the fingers until it assumes the desired shape. This method is best suited for making small or medium-sized forms. Although pinch pots are often round, they may assume any shape your fingers wish to give them. A round form may be paddled with a board or patted with your hands to modify its shape. Pinch pots may be modeled long (like a cucumber) or asymetrically rather than round. Pinching is a good technique to use in making small simple clay figures. Since the entire figure is made from one lump of clay, and the arms, legs, and head are "pinched" from the mass, it is a one-step operation—that is, it requires no scoring or adding of parts. This is an excellent method to use with children for making small animal shapes.

Pinch pots of different sizes are made by using a slight variation of the same technique. To make a small pot, the clay ball is held in the palm of one hand (the left, if you are right-handed), while the fingers of the other hand do the forming. The clay is pinched between the thumb and fingers of the right hand. To make a larger pinch pot, the clay is

Teapot made by pinch pot technique. It is 6 inches high and was made in 1959 by Clayton Bailey. *(Photo courtesy of the artist)*

set down on a bat, piece of tinfoil, or paper towel so it may be moved around. (A turntable facilitates this process since it revolves.) The clay is pinched between the thumbs and fingers of both hands.

Clay used for making pinch pots should be fine-grained. If grog is added, this should also be fine-grained. The clay should be well wedged. It should also be moist enough so that it is easy to shape and does not require constant sponging, yet not so wet that it does not hold its shape. Since clay dries out with repeated hand contact, it is best to try to complete your piece as quickly as possible, before the clay becomes too "tired" and dry and too many cracks appear. If the pot does develop small cracks, pressing them together and smoothing with your fingers will usually blend them successfully into the clay. If large cracks appear, these will become more pronounced in drying; the clay should be rewedged and the procedure begun anew with a fresh moist piece.

BASIC PINCH POTS

MATERIALS
Bat, piece of tin foil, or paper towel
Turntable (optional)

Step 1: Take a piece of moist, wedged clay about the size of your fist. Roll it into a round ball.

Step 2: Place the clay ball on a damp bat (or turntable if you have one), piece of tin foil, or paper towel.

Step 3: Push your thumb down into the middle of the ball to make a hole that reaches almost to its bottom. Leave about ⅜ to ½ inch of clay at the bottom.

Step 4: Now widen the hole by sticking your other thumb into it. Holding the rest of your fingers around the sides of the clay ball, push toward them with your thumbs. This will widen the hole still further so that you can begin shaping the pot. If you find that your hands are sticking to the clay, wet them slightly before continuing work. Do this whenever it seems necessary. However, do not saturate the piece with too much water—this weakens the clay.

Step 5: Still keeping your thumbs on the inside of the bowl and your fingers on the outside, "pinch" the clay between your thumbs and fingers. Turn the pot around slowly each time you squeeze so that it will be even all around. Brace the walls of the pot by cupping your fingers around them. Pinch the clay upward and you will see the piece become taller in shape, while its walls grow thinner. Push the clay outward (by pressing harder on the inside walls of the pot) and you will see it become wider and thinner. The way the pot develops is completely up to you. Your fingers determine its shape and thickness.

Step 6: Try to make the pot as uniform in thickness as possible. Do not leave too much clay at the bottom sides or make the top edges too thin (the two most common mistakes made by beginners). Move the clay up and out of the bottom area where the sides of the pot begin. Leave the rim the same thickness as the rest of the clay wall, or even thicken it a bit. If you feel the rim getting too thin, fold the top over the outside edge and work it into the rest of the clay. If a pot is much thinner in one area and thicker in another, it will dry unevenly and probably crack.

Step 7: If the pot begins to show signs of cracking, you may be working too slowly. Try to speed up a bit. Pinch small cracks together with your fingers and smooth with a damp sponge.

Step 8: After you have completed your shape, let it dry until it is almost leather-hard. Then smooth out any bumps and pat it into its final form. The pot may be turned upside down to flatten the rim and allowed to dry in this manner. A small clay coil may be attached to the bottom of the pot to form a foot. Score the coil and the area of the pot where it will be joined. Attach with slip.

Step 9: Allow the pot to dry thoroughly. Fire and glaze as desired.

BOWLS, ASHTRAYS, AND VASES

To make a bowl, ashtray, or vase follow the general instructions for making pinch pots. The size of the piece will depend upon the amount of clay used. The pinch method is best suited for small to medium-sized clay pieces. It is generally not used for tall forms since the pot is made all at one time and the clay will only stand to a certain height without buckling. It is however possible to make larger forms in this manner provided that they are built at several work sessions and that the clay is allowed to firm up between additions. This is done by making a 4- to 6-inch pot, covering the rim with plastic so that it stays moist enough for subsequent additions and allowing the rest of the pot to air dry for an hour or two before adding more clay. Then a large thick slab or coil is added to the existing form, and this is pinched into shape to harmonize with the rest of the piece. This process may be repeated several times. For initial experiences it is recommended that pinching be used only for making smaller pieces that can be created at one sitting.

It is possible to use this method to make low wide forms such as bowls or fairly large ash trays. As you experiment with different sizes and shapes, you will find out which are most suitable for this technique.

Raku pinch bowl made by Linda Pierce. (Photograph by Howard M. Berliant)

Bowls

MATERIALS
Same as for basic pinch pots

Step 1: Begin with a ball of wedged clay. The larger the ball, the larger the finished bowl.

Step 2: Follow the general directions for making pinch pots. If you want your bowl to be low and wide, push the sides out with your thumbs, using your outside fingers to support the wall. Continue pushing out rather than up, until you have the shape you want. If you are making a taller, narrower bowl, pull up with your fingers while pushing out. Turn the bowl as you work so that it will be of even thickness all around.

Pinch pot ash trays by the author. (Photograph by Howard M. Berliant)

Ashtrays

MATERIALS
Sharp knife

Step 1: To make an ashtray, first make a low bowl. Allow it to dry until it is leather-hard.

Step 2: After smoothing the surface, cut one, two, or three notches (u- or v-shaped) into the rim with

a sharp knife. Make the notches somewhat larger than cigarette size. (Remember that clay shrinks.) Smooth them with a damp sponge.

Step 3: When making an ashtray, it is especially important that the rim be at least as thick as the rest of the piece. Since this is the part on which the most stress is placed, it may even be a bit thicker.

Textured pinch pot vase by Michele Cole *(Photograph by Howard M. Berliant)*

Vases

MATERIALS
Same as for basic pinch pots

A first vase made by pinching should be fairly small and simple. Before beginning, decide upon the shape you wish to make. It is better to have something in mind (even if you fall short of your goal) than to "just see what happens." A high bowl shape, curving in at the top rather than flaring out, is a good choice. In choosing a shape, remember that the function of a vase is to hold flowers but that it is also a decorative piece.

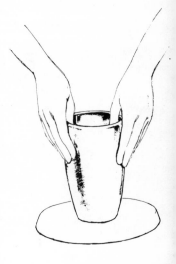

Step 1: Shape a piece of wedged clay about the size of an orange into a round ball.

Step 2: Follow the general directions for pinch pots, making the form tall and narrow rather than short and wide.

Step 3: In shaping the clay, pinch the walls upward between your thumbs and fingers, lifting the clay rather than pushing it out.

Step 4: If you want the neck of the vase to be narrower than the base, begin bringing the clay in gradually from the widest point by pressure from the outside. Curves that are too exaggerated often cause the clay to collapse. To keep the top from getting too wide, exert most of the pressure on the clay from the outside with your fingers. Use your thumbs mainly to support the walls from the inside.

Note: A general rule to remember (though there are always exceptions): Vases go in; most of the pressure is exerted from the outside. Bowls go out; most of the pressure is exerted from the inside.

Pinch pot bells suspended from driftwood by le[ather]
thongs. Made by Vera Kranz. *(Photograph by H*[?]
M. Berliant)

BELLS

MATERIALS
Cutting wire
Sharp knife or trimming tool
Nail
Bat
Leather thong, twine, or string for hanging

Clay bells are musical and simple to make and
provide effective visual and auditory enhancement
to a patio or porch. They are made by forming a
bell-shaped vase, turning it upside down, making
a hole through the top of the bell, and suspending
a clapper inside it.

Before you begin making bells, consider some variations upon the conventional bell shape or at least modify the orthodox form in size or width. Make a long, thin bell, or a short, fat one. Try one with edges that curve in rather than flare out. Use a simple shape. It is often best to sketch a few shapes on paper before actually beginning to work in clay.

Follow the steps listed for making a basic pinch pot. Work on a bat, placed on a turntable if you have one. There will be two slight differences from the basic procedure.

Step 1: You will be working on the bell upside down. In other words, you will proceed as if you were making a flared-top pinch pot vase. When the vase is turned upside down and suspended from a string, it will magically turn into a bell.

Step 2: When making a bowl, vase, ashtray, or any object that supports itself, you should give it a flat bottom so that it will stand securely. In this case, you may not want a flat bottom, since the bottom will actually be the top of the bell, and the top of a bell is often rounded. (Always keep in mind what the finished product will look like while you are working with clay.)

Step 3: After you have completed the form, allow it to dry until it is almost leather-hard. Then remove the bell from the bat by slicing it off with a cutting wire. You may want to modify the shape of what is now the top of the bell by trimming away excess clay to give a more conical shape to the top, or perhaps to emphasize a flat top. Make any corrections in shape with a trimming tool or a sharp knife.

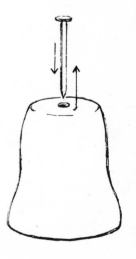

Step 4: Poke a hole through the top of the bell with a sharp nail. Make sure the hole is large enough to accommodate a cord, thong, or some sort of device for hanging the finished bell.

Step 5: Smooth any rough spots with a damp sponge. Check the rim for cracks or unevenness.

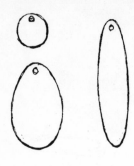

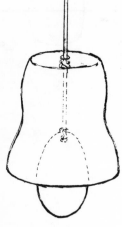

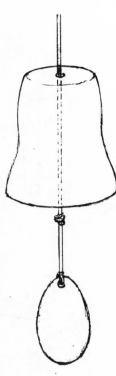

At this stage, you may want to decorate the clay by incising designs into it.

Step 6: Make a clapper. One way to do this is to make a large clay bead that will hit against the side of the bell as it moves. A clapper may also be made by cutting shapes from rolled-out clay (as in making jewelry). When the clapper is leather-hard, make a hole in it with a sharp nail so it may be attached to the bell.

Step 7: Allow the bell and clapper to dry thoroughly. Fire and glaze (or leave unglazed, glaze only the outside, etc.) as desired.

Step 8: Attach the fired clapper to one end of a fairly long piece of cord, thong, or wire. Run the cord up to the top of the bell so that the clapper hangs (and hits) near the bottom of the bell. Part of it should protrude from the bell.

Step 9: With a pencil or crayon, make a mark on the string at the point where it comes out of the bell hole.

Step 10: Now remove the string and make several knots at the place where the pencil mark is.

Step 11: When you put the string through again, the bell hole will rest on the knot and the clapper will ring against the bottom sides of the bell. (If you had no knot, or your knot was too small, the clapper would slip to the top of the bell and not be able to perform its function of ringing.)

Step 12: Cut the string to desired length and hang the bell outside on your porch or patio. Several bells of various shapes and sizes will provide pleasant sights and sounds when the wind blows.

Garden goblin made from two pinch pots.
By the author. (Photograph by Howard M. Berliant)

GARDEN GOBLINS

MATERIALS
Knife or sharp tool
Bat
Slip
Thin sheet of plastic or plastic bag
Clay that fires to a pleasing color at bisque tem-
perature

Garden goblins are whimsical creatures for use
in an outdoor setting, such as a garden or patio.
They are easily made by joining two pinch pots
together and attaching legs to them. Features may
be added to vary the basic shape. Children especially enjoy this project when encouraged to make
their creations as goblin-spooky or goblin-funny as
they wish.

The instructions given here will make a small
goblin. Of course size may be varied according to
taste. Groups of goblins in varieties of sizes and

shapes make an unusual focal point in an outdoor area.

Step 1: For each part of the goblin, use a ball of clay about the size of a tennis ball. (You may use a slightly smaller ball for the head and one a bit larger for the body.) Make each ball into a tallish bowl.

Step 2: Let the bowls dry until they are almost leather-hard. As in making bells, try not to make too flat a bottom on your bowls.

Step 3: Turn one bowl (the smaller one if there is a size difference) upside down. Make features from tiny pieces of clay and attach them to the face with slip. Or incise features with a knife or sharp tool.

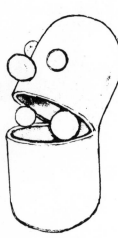

Step 4: Using a bat or board as a working surface, stack the face bowl on top of the body bowl, and then tilt the face bowl backward a bit, so that there is an opening between face and body bowl. Place a small clay ball at the sides of the opening to keep the pieces apart while drying.

Step 5: Attach the top bowl to the bottom bowl at the back by scoring the rim of both bowls where they are to be joined. Apply slip to the scored parts and push the parts together.

Step 6: Roll a long coil of clay (or two shorter ones) for the legs and attach it in back at the joint of the two pots. When fastening the clay coil, score it and the area of the pot where it will be attached. Let the coil extend all around the back of the body and to the sides. Bend the coils into feet at the bottom.

Step 7: Smooth the entire form with a slightly damp sponge, wiping away any excess slip that may have oozed from junctures. Be sure all sections are securely attached.

Step 8: Cover the piece with a sheet of thin plastic and allow it to dry slowly. While it is drying, check it frequently to see that no cracks develop (since wetter clay was joined to drier clay and since all parts may not be the same thickness). Smooth small cracks with your fingers and a damp sponge. When the piece is fairly dry, the plastic may be removed and the goblin allowed to air dry.

Step 9: Fire when thoroughly dry. Since goblins will be used outdoors, the natural clay color is generally quite attractive when bisque-fired and left unglazed. Succulents or other small growing things may be planted in the goblin's belly.

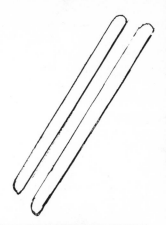

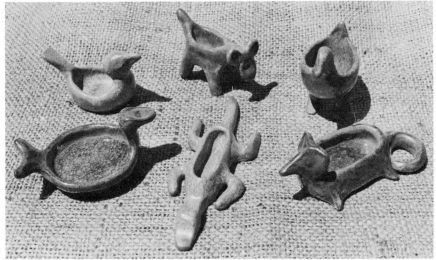

Pinch pot animals. Some of these animals are pinched from one piece of clay. Others, like the alligator and mouse, have small pieces attached which are then modeled into proper shape (tails, legs, etc.). Made by Anni Grundler. *(Photograph by Howard M. Berliant)*

PINCH POT ANIMALS

Pinch pot animals may be used as decorative non-functional pieces or they can carry a candle on their back or hold a small wad of florist's clay embedded with tiny straw flowers. They may be used as fishbowl ornaments, holders to serve small candies or nuts, or miniature ash trays.

Some simple animal shapes particularly suited to

this method of construction are turtles, ducks, birds, mice, and fish. Each one can be made from one piece of clay. For other animals, modeled parts may be added to the basic form.

The directions below are for a pinch pot turtle. The same method may be used for other animals. Simply vary the features in accordance with the animal you are creating. These pots are most attractive when made quite small.

Small Pinch Pot Turtle

MATERIALS
Small plastic bag

Step 1: Take a lump of wedged clay about the size of a golf ball and roll it between your palms until it is smooth and round.

Step 2: Push your thumb into the middle and make a hole directly in the center of the ball. Since this will be a tiny pinch pot, you do not need to use both hands to shape the clay. Hold the clay in the palm of your left hand and squeeze it between the thumb and first two fingers of the right hand. In other words, pinch! (Reverse hands if you are left-handed.) As in two-handed pinching, the thumb is usually on the inside, the fingers on the outside, but the process may be reversed at times. Turn the pot slowly in your left palm as you work on it. Make the pot low and wide rather than high. This one-hand method is suitable for any small pinch forms. When you are working with a piece of clay that is golf-ball size or smaller, this technique should be used rather than the two-handed method. Between golf-ball and tennis-ball size, either method may be used. For larger pieces, the two-hand process is more suitable.

Step 3: To make a turtle, pinch a tiny piece of clay at one end of the finished pot into a head. Now pinch four feet from the bottom sides of the pot. If you wish, pinch a tiny tail from the end opposite the head. Smooth and shape the form until it is completed to your satisfaction.

Step 4: Cover the turtle with a small plastic bag and allow it to dry slowly. Here again the piece is made of thicker and thinner parts, so differences in drying time must be diminished and compensated for as much as possible. Watch for cracks, especially around head and feet, and smooth with a damp sponge any that develop.

Step 5: Allow the turtle to dry slowly. Fire and glaze.

8

COIL POTS

There are many different ways to make hand-built pottery. The pinch method, discussed in the previous chapter, is especially suitable for making small pots. Another technique for forming pottery is the coil method. Thousands of years before the potter's wheel was invented, this was used to form round, symmetrical shapes. While the coil method is also suited to making small pots, it is equally adaptable to larger forms.

Coiling consists of rolling out "ropes" or coils of clay and layering these on top of one another. This technique lends itself well to the talents of both the novice and advanced craftsman. (Though a little practice is required to roll uniform coils, it is a skill that can be readily learned.) It provides an opportunity to make shapes simulating those created on the wheel, yet using only the potter's hands to shape the clay into the desired form. Coil pottery does not have to be either round or symmetrical. Many interesting departures from the round shape are possible (oval, irregular, even square creations) once the basic technique has been mastered. In fact, coiling allows the potter freedom to create forms not as easily achieved by other methods. For example, since coil pots do not have to be completed at one sitting, it is possible to make very large pieces using this method—adding on section by section over a period of time—provided of course that each section is allowed to stiffen sufficiently to support the weight of the clay built upon it. Coiling is also an excellent method for working with coarse groggy clays, which are ill-suited for use on the potter's wheel yet lend themselves well to this technique.

Coil-building, by its very nature, provides interesting surface texture. The coils themselves provide the piece with inherent design. Of course it is not necessary to leave the coils showing. They can be completely or partially "erased" by smoothing the form by hand or with a wooden tool, rib, rubber kidney, spoon back, and so on. Interesting variations may be achieved by a combination of smooth and coiled textures—that is, by "erasing" some coils and leaving others intact.

For working in the coil method, the clay should be quite plastic, but not wet. Since each coil is rolled by hand, this has a drying effect upon the clay. If the coils become too dry during the rolling-out process, they will crack. If the clay is too wet, the coils will stretch or become distorted in shape when they are lifted from the working surface to the form under construction.

In making coiled pottery, a turntable is especially useful, since it allows the piece to revolve without constant handling as you are working on it. If it is not possible to avail yourself of a turntable, work on a damp bat, piece of tin foil, or any device that will allow you to move the piece without picking it up.

The size and thickness of the base and coils will vary depending upon the size of the piece you are making. In any technique of forming clay, size and thickness should always relate harmoniously. A small coil pot would have a thinner base and smaller, thinner coils than a larger form. If your piece were 3- or 4-inches high, the coils might be ¼ inch in diameter and the base ¼- to ⅜-inch thick. For a larger piece—say 8- or 9-inches high—the base would be about ½-inch thick and the coils ½ inch in diameter. Pot thickness (in this case, coil thickness) generally increases in relation to size. The larger the piece, the thicker the coils.

When joining coils, do not place the joint of the coil ends (where coils meet) on top of each other—that is, the ends of one coil should not go on the ends of the one beneath it. Try to space the coil joints around the pot. If they all meet in the same area, that side of the pot will tend to be weakened.

BASIC COIL POTS—CYLINDERS

The cylinder is the basic (and easiest) form to make by this method. Since each coil is placed directly on the one preceding it, this is a good first project for learning the fundamental technique of coiling. Make your first cylinder small to medium in size.

MATERIALS
Knife or sharp tool
Drinking glass, cookie-cutter, or round pattern for base of pot
Banding wheel, damp bat, or tin foil
Rolling pin
Slip
Plastic sheeting

Step 1: Begin with a lump of wedged clay that seems suitable in size for the form you wish to make. Break off a small piece of the clay and roll it with a rolling pin to about ¼- to ½-inch thickness. Using a cookie-cutter, the open end of a drinking glass, or paper pattern, cut a round circle from the clay. This will serve as the base of your coil pot.

Step 2: Break off another small piece of clay and roll it between your palms into a fat, sausage-shaped cylinder.

Step 3: Place this "fat coil" on your work surface and roll it back and forth, pressing down on it lightly with your palms, keeping your fingers outstretched. Roll the coil from the center toward the ends, moving your palms out from the middle as you go. This lengthens and thins the coil. The coil may also be rolled by using the fingers rather than the palms of the hands—again working out from the middle, spreading your fingers slightly as you roll the clay. With either method try to keep the coil of uniform thickness throughout. If the coil begins to crack, the working surface (oilcloth, etc.)

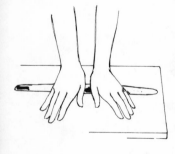

should be lightly sprinkled with water—not too much or the clay will stick.

Step 4: Roll several coils at a time. Four or five is a good number. They may be covered with plastic to keep them from drying out.

Step 5: Measure the coil to fit the base. To do this, lay a coil on the base to form a circle. Cut off excess clay where the coil ends overlap. For this project, other coils may be cut to match the first coil—since, in a straight cylinder, all coils are the same size.

Step 6: Score the edge of the base with a knife or sharp tool. Scratch into the clay first in one direction, then in the other. Moisten the scoring with a damp sponge. Score the bottom and two cut ends of the first coil. In making coil pots, scoring is most important, unless the coils are very moist, since so many separate parts are joined. If each coil is not sufficiently scored and blended into the one below it, the coils may separate while drying or, in the process of firing, cause the piece to crack.

Step 7: Lay the first coil, scored side down, on the scored edge of the base and press the coil lightly onto the base. Place a little slip on the cut ends of the coils and join them together.

Step 8: On the inside of the form, work the clay down from the coil into the base with a wooden modeling tool or your fingers. Make sure the coil is firmly joined to the base. Smooth with your fingers. Repeat this process on the outside, blending the first coil into the base.

Step 9: Score the bottom and cut ends of coil number 2. Score the top of coil 1 (which is already on the pot). Put slip on top of the first coil. Press the second coil, scored side down, on the first coil. Some slip may ooze out of the space between the coils. Wipe this away with a damp sponge. The slip placed on the scored parts acts like glue, causing the coils to stick to one another.

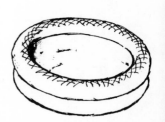

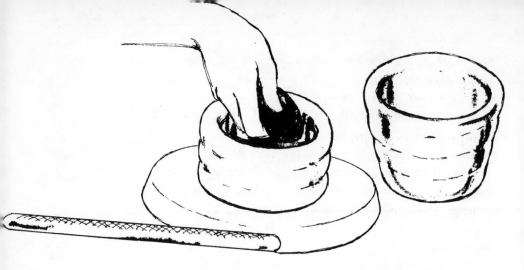

Step 10: Work some clay down from coil number 2 into the area between coils 1 and 2, smoothing the clay firmly with your fingers. If you wish to leave the texture of the pot intact, work this and succeeding coils into each other only from the inside. (A little smoothing may be done on the outside of the pot, but be careful not to disturb the shape of the coils.) If you wish to eliminate the texture, work the coils into each other from both inside and outside.

Step 11: Continue in this manner until you have placed four or five coils on top of each other. Allow the piece to dry for an hour or two before adding more coils. If the clay is not allowed to firm up about every four or five coils, the form may collapse. The amount of coils added each time and the time needed for the piece to firm up will vary, depending on the size of the piece and thickness of the coils used.

Step 12: After the pot has stiffened sufficiently, more coils may be added (about four or five again) without fear of buckling. The top coil should be covered with a sheet of thin plastic while the piece is drying so that it does not become too stiff for successful joining. For a first project, eight to ten coils is a suitable, easy-to-work-with height. As you advance, you may add coils to greater height, working over a period of days, if necessary, to complete the project.

Step 13: Allow the pot to dry slowly. You may want to cover it with a plastic bag initially and then allow it to air dry. Fire and glaze.

Note: When working with very moist coils, it is not necessary to score and use slip, especially if the coils will be blended both on the inside and outside of the form. Each moist coil may be placed on top of the one below it and firmly blended with your fingers.

Coil vase with impressed finger decoration. Anni Grundler. *(Photograph by Howard M. Berliant)*

BOWLS AND VASES

The coil method is an excellent technique for making bowls and vases of almost any size. It is easy to get a variety of shapes by changing the length of the coils used. In the cylinder we have just discussed, all the coils were made the same size and placed directly on top of one another. In a bowl that flares out, the coils are made progressively longer and each is placed on the outer rim of the one beneath it. In a vase that curves inward, the coils are made progressively smaller and each is placed on the inner rim of the one beneath it. So the shape of the pot is determined by the size of the coils and their placement.

Bowls

MATERIALS
Same as for cylinder
Rubber kidney or wooden rib

Step 1: To make a bowl that is wider at the top than at the bottom, first cut a base just as you would for a cylinder.

Step 2: Roll a coil to fit the base, plus four or five longer coils for the body of the piece. These may be trimmed to size later. Cover the extra coils with plastic to keep them from becoming too dry. Join the first coil to the base as stated in the general directions. The techniques that you follow in making a bowl will be the same as for a cylinder. The only difference will be the length and placement of the coils.

Step 3: Trim the second coil so that it is a bit longer than the first coil. Now place it on the outer edge of the first coil, working the clay between the coils with your fingers. Cut the third coil, again a bit longer than the second coil, and again place it on the outer edge of the coil beneath it. Coils are made in advance but cut to fit as they are stacked upon one another. Be sure to score the coils and use slip just as you did when making the cylinder. Each succeeding coil should be somewhat longer than the one beneath it until the bowl has reached its desired height and form.

Step 4: Allow the clay to firm up between additions if you plan to use more than four or five coils.

Step 5: The inside of the bowl may be smoothed

with a wooden rib or rubber kidney to obtain a more even interior and eliminate finger marks.

Step 6: Complete as per general directions.

Templates

In constructing a form such as a vase you may want to use a template to guide its shape. A template is a pattern cut from cardboard in the silhouette of the finished piece. When it is placed adjacent to the pot under construction, it is easy to make the piece conform to its contours. While it is by no means necessary, or even advisable, to use templates for all coil pots, they are often helpful for pieces that depend on symmetry for good design or in controlling the contours of large pieces. They are most useful when making a matched set of mugs or bowls.

To make a template, draw the form in the size and shape you plan for your finished product on a sheet of paper. Cut it out. Fold this cut form in half and transfer the half design to a piece of cardboard. Cut the silhouette from the cardboard, leaving enough room at the top of the template so it can be easily held. Place the template adjacent to the pot as coils are added. See that the shape of the pot fits the curves of the template. Use the template to check the shape of all the sides of the pot. Correct any discrepancies.

Vases

MATERIALS
Same as for cylinder
Template (optional)

The directions given here are for making a vase without the aid of a template, but a template may be used as a guide to match the coils against the pattern.

Step 1: To make a vase that "bellies" in the middle, make the base relatively small. Then proceed as for a bowl, making each coil a bit longer than the one beneath it and placing each on the outer edge of the coil below it.

Step 2: When you reach the point where the vase goes out furthest, make a few coils all the same size and place them directly on top of each other as for a cylinder. This will be the "belly" of the vase. After this bulge, the vase will begin to get narrower.

Step 3: To make the pot go in, coils are made progressively shorter. Each coil is placed just a little to the inside of the one beneath it. Continue in this manner (making each coil somewhat shorter than the one below it and putting each one on the inner edge of the one beneath it) until the vase has reached its desired size and shape.

Step 4: Again, be sure to allow the form to stiffen sufficiently about every five rows. Complete as for general directions.

You can, of course, vary the shape of the vase in any manner by making the coils go in or out. Remember, coils of increasing length placed on the outside edge of those beneath them cause the pot to flare out. Coils of decreasing length placed on the inside edge of the ones beneath them cause the pot to curve in.

Large coil pot with coils laid in designs in the upper section. Here coils are used both as methods of construction and as methods of design. Diana Bohn. *(Photograph by Howard M. Berliant)*

LARGE POTS

If you plan to make a very large pot, it is best to allow several days for the procedure since the clay may "buckle" if it is built up too high when wet.

MATERIALS
Same as for cylinder
Template (optional)
Wooden rib or rubber kidney (optional)

Step 1: Make a base and several long, thick coils. Build to the height of four or five coils as in general directions. If the clay shows no signs of stress, add a few more. How many coils can be added will depend on the size and thickness of the coils and the wetness of the clay.

Step 2: Cover the top coil with plastic and let the piece dry for several hours. Or cover the entire form very loosely with plastic and let it dry over night between additions.

Step 3: Continue this procedure according to general directions. Here again you may wish to use a template in controlling the shape of the pot, especially if the form is to be symmetrical or varies greatly in contour.

PIECES WITH HANDLES

Handles are for holding. The main function of a handle is to make the piece easier to grasp. A container without a handle may be suitable for cold drinks but is not very comfortable to hold when filled with hot coffee. A handle solves this problem. A large pitcher is easier to pour if it has a handle. A casserole with a long handle on one

Coil teapots with handles. Deborah Kaufman. *(Photograph by Howard M. Berliant)*

side or two short ones on either end is simpler to carry. The main thing to remember when making handles is to make them strong enough to grasp properly and to attach them firmly so they will not break away from the sides of the pot. When attaching handles, always be sure to score the piece well, use adequate amounts of slip, and work the handle into the pot securely. Make a handle that relates to the rest of the piece both in proportion and style.

Coiled Handles

For a coil pot, the most suitable handle might also be a coil. A coil may be used in its simplest form, or two or three coils may be laid side by side or interwoven.

Step 1: Finish the pot to which the handle will be attached.

Step 2: Make a coil as if you were rolling it for the pot. Study the piece and decide on appropriate size and shape for the handle.

Step 3: Bend the coil into the desired shape and cut to approximate length.

Step 4: Allow the pot and the coil to dry to the leather-hard stage.

Step 5: Cut the handle to the right length and score both ends. Score the areas on the pot where it is to be attached. Put slip on the scorings. Attach the handle firmly at the scored points, working it into the piece with a wooden modeling tool. Make sure the handle adheres to the pot. Make a small clay coil and place it around the joint area. This will help to strengthen the joint further. If a handle is not firmly attached, it may come off the main piece while the pot is drying or during the firing process. Since the handle absorbs the main stress when the pot is in use, it may also separate from the finished piece.

Step 6: Work the small coil into the joint and smooth the clay with your fingers. You may use a damp sponge to eliminate any unevenness.

Slab-building is another ancient pottery technique that provides interesting variations from the methods discussed thus far. While pinching and coiling are generally thought of as techniques for producing round forms or variations upon this theme, the slab method is an ideal way of constructing flat or geometric shapes. Square, rectangular, and asymmetrical straight-sided pieces are particularly suitable for slab-building—and perhaps more freely and easily made by this method than any other. In making geometric straight-sided forms, the slabs are generally allowed to stiffen until they can be easily handled without damage before they are joined. Many textured slabs may be used to create interesting free-form pieces.

Slab construction allows great variety in departures from round forms. Of course it is also possible to make cylindrical pieces from slabs, provided that the slabs are sufficiently plastic to be easily bent without cracking. For making large cylindrical hand-built pottery, the coil method is often preferable to the slab.

Slab-building, as its name implies, uses "slabs" of clay—rolled out, pounded, or sliced to uniform thickness, which are joined together to form a finished construction. Some craftsmen cut large slabs from a clay block with the aid of a strong cutting wire. Others merely pound the clay flat with their

9

SLAB POTS

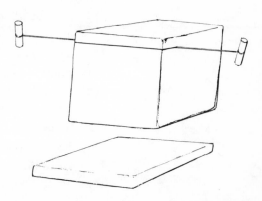

hands, using the slightly uneven texture as part of the design of the finished piece. Depending on the sort of piece you are making, working the clay with your hands alone may suit your purposes well at times. At others, you will want the more exact proportions that careful rolling and cutting provides. Therefore, it is recommended that you practice the procedure of rolling the clay with a rolling pin, employing two guide sticks to ensure uniform thickness, and use this method in your initial slab work.

The tiles and trivets included in Chapter 6 are simple slab pieces, using just one slab to form the finished product. The basic tile form—that is, a single slab—may be modified in other ways to form simple contoured pieces. For more complicated forms, several slabs are welded together to construct a piece of desired shape.

Almost any type of clay may be used in slab-building. Since flat pieces often have a tendency to warp, it is recommended that grog be wedged into the clay used for platters, plates, or other flat forms, particularly if the clay you will be using is fine-grained. Depending on the size, thickness, and ultimate function of the piece, 10 percent to 15 percent grog may be added and up to 20 percent for very flat constructions like plates or tiles. Be sure that any clay used for slab-building is well-wedged.

In slab-building, there are two basic variations in method: (1) soft slab construction, as used here for slab trays and sling pieces, and (2) leather-hard slab construction, as used for other projects in this section. Soft slabs are employed primarily for pieces that will be supported as they dry, usually by a sling, coils, or a mold of some sort. The clay may be soft because it does not have to support its own weight. While the soft slab technique is suitable for making pieces from one slab of clay, the leather-hard method is more versatile, allowing for the construction of forms with many pieces rather than just one.

Slabs should be allowed to dry until they are almost leather-hard if you are making a straight-sided construction. In the leather-hard technique, building with slabs is related to carpentry, except that slip and scoring are used to hold the piece together instead of nails. If the slab is to be curved, it must be wet enough to bend without cracking yet should still be firm enough to be handled without distorting its shape (between soft and leather-hard). Slabs that are too wet will lose their shape, causing the pot to collapse under construction. Slabs are joined to each other by means of scoring and the addition of slip. Small coils may be placed at the junctures and blended with the fingers to further ensure adhesion.

SLAB TRAYS OR PLATES
(Soft slab method)

MATERIALS
Paper pattern in the shape of the piece
Rolling pin
Two wooden guide sticks about ⅜- to ½-inch thick
Sharp knife
Thin sheet of plastic

Slab tray. By Michi Zimmerman. (Photograph by Howard M. Berliant)

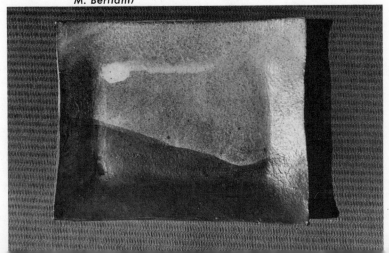

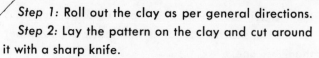

Step 1: Roll out the clay as per general directions.

Step 2: Lay the pattern on the clay and cut around it with a sharp knife.

Step 3: Allow the slab to "rest" until it is firm enough to handle. Now transfer it to a plaster bat or some other surface where it may remain undisturbed until it becomes leather-hard.

Step 4: Roll several coils of uniform thickness and position them under the edges of the slab. This will serve to turn the edges upward. The thickness of the coils used will depend on the amount of curve you wish the edges to have. A coil about ½ inch in diameter will raise the edges gently. (Vary the thickness of the coils according to personal preference.) Press the sides of the slab lightly against the coils. The coils will support the edges while they are drying and should be left until the piece is leather-hard. If they are removed before the clay has dried sufficiently the sides will droop.

Step 5: Allow the piece to dry to the leather-hard stage. Discard the coils. Remove excess clay that may have adhered to the slab from the coils. Trim any unevenness from the edges of the plate with a knife or trimming tool and smooth with a damp sponge.

Step 6: Transfer the piece to a damp bat. Cover with a sheet of thin plastic and allow to dry slowly to minimize warping.

Step 7: Fire and glaze.

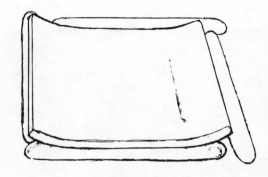

Slab platter, with foot. Made by the sling method by Michele Cole. (Photograph by Howard M. Berliant)

SLING PIECES—PLATTER
(Soft slab method)

MATERIALS
Pattern for platter
Rolling pin
Guide sticks
Sharp knife
Corrugated paper (or other large) box
Clothespins
Burlap, canvas, or oilcloth

A sling piece is made from one slab of moist clay, cut to desired shape, and "slung" or suspended in a "hammock" of some sort. A corrugated paper box with a piece of burlap or canvas fastened to it with clothespins makes a good hammock. The fabric is adjusted to hang inside the box. Clothespins are used as fasteners. If the cloth is secured fairly tautly the piece will have only a slight curve. This is a simple way of making a shallow platter. If the material is fastened loosely, the curve will be greater. This is a good method for making a low bowl or serving dish. The curve of the piece will be in direct proportion to the curve of the sling.

Slab sculptures. Sculpture on right is perforated around one edge. Nylon string is laced through the holes into a design. It is often effective to combine clay with another material such as string, leather, wood, or with another technique such as macramé or weaving. Sculptures by Anni Grundler. (Photograph by Howard M. Berliant)

First make a hammock or sling.

Step 1: Use a corrugated paper box somewhat larger than the size of your finished piece.

Step 2: Cut a piece of burlap or canvas about four inches larger on all sides than the box. (A rough material such as burlap provides interesting texture for the bottom of the piece. Its roughness also prevents the clay from sticking to it.)

Step 3: Fasten the burlap to the edge of the box with clothespins. The amount of "slack" in the cloth will depend on the curve you want the piece to have. If you are making a platter with only a shallow curve, fasten the cloth to sag slightly. If you want a deeper dish, loosen the cloth so it sags more.

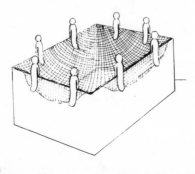

Step 4: Set the sling in the approximate curve you want. It may be adjusted further after you place the clay piece inside it.

Sling Pieces

Step 1: Draw a pattern of the shape on a piece of cardboard or heavy paper. Be sure to make the pattern somewhat larger than your finished piece will be because, as always, the clay will shrink and, when the piece is curved, it will appear smaller than when it is flat. Cut out the pattern.

Step 2: Roll out a slab of the proper size, on oilcloth, burlap, or canvas. Place paper pattern upon it, and cut around it with a sharp knife.

Step 3: Allow the clay to firm up just until it can be moved without damage (it should still be soft). Lift the slab carefully and place it gently in the center of the sling.

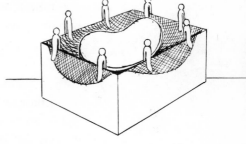

Step 4: If the slab does not assume the proper contours, tighten or loosen the burlap, one clothespin at a time, until the desired effect is achieved.

Step 5: Cover the piece loosely with plastic sheeting and allow it to dry until it is leather-hard.

Step 6: Remove the piece from the sling, smooth it slightly with a damp sponge, checking especially for roughness around the edges. The edges may be textured at this time. If the piece is to be used to hold food, it is best not to make any incised designs in the area where food will be put. Otherwise, the food may stick to the depressions and the piece will be hard to clean.

Step 7: Because of its built-in curve, the sling pot may not stand stably on a flat surface. Therefore, it is advisable to give it some sort of base or "foot." This can be done in a number of ways. Here are a few suggestions:

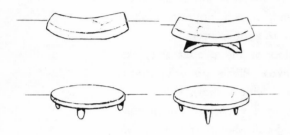

(a) With a sharp knife, slice the curve of the bottom so that it is flat enough to allow the piece to stand without wobbling. Smooth with a damp sponge.

(b) Make a coil or two. Turn the sling piece upside down and attach coils to the underside of the form. Score and use slip according to the procedure for making coil pots.

(c) Model three or four small feet by hand and attach them in the proper places (as when making trivets) so that the pot looks attractive and stands securely.

(d) Make a shallow pinch pot, turn it upside down and attach it to the sling piece when both are leather-hard.

(e) Of course a slab pot may also have a slab foot. You might make a smaller form in the same shape as your platter and sling it. When both are leather-hard, attach the small one upside down as a base for the large one.

Three straight slabs may be used to form a triangular base, a curved slab to form a round or oval base, and so on. Slab bases may be made in any form that suits the design of the platter.

Step 8: After making a base or feet, again cover the piece loosely with plastic and allow it to dry slowly.

Step 9: Fire and glaze.

Slab box with foot and flanged lid with handle. Raku fired. Made by Andrée Thompson. (Photograph by Howard M. Berliant)

BOXES

MATERIALS
Paper pattern for each section of box—4 sides, base (and lid if desired)
Ruler
Rolling pin
Two wooden guide sticks ⅜- to ½-inch thick
Sharp knife
Thin sheet of plastic

Step 1: Roll out the clay as per general directions.

Step 2: Make a pattern for each section of the box from paper or lightweight cardboard; 3 by 5 or 5 by 5 inches is a good size for the first attempt. If the base is 5 by 5 inches, two sides of the box will be 5 inches long and the other two 4 inches (taking into account the thickness of the clay—assuming in this case that the slabs are ½-inch thick). If the box is 3 by 5 inches, two sides will be 3-inches long while the other two are 4 inches—or two may be 2 inches while the others are 5 inches. The walls will be placed on top of the base rather than around it. (If you wish to place the walls around rather than on the base, two walls would have to be 1-inch longer than the base—that is a 3-by-5-inch base would require two walls 3-inches and two 6-inches long—or two 4 inches and 2 five inches—again because of the thickness of the slabs themselves.)

The slabs may be 2, 3, 4, or more inches tall, as long as all are the same height. Height may vary according to your taste and the function of the form. If you wish to make a lid for the box, make a pattern piece the same size as the base. If you do not plan to use a pattern, work out the exact measurements of the box and use a ruler to measure the slab shapes directly on the clay with a pencil or a sharp tool.

Step 3: Cut around the measured slabs with a sharp knife.

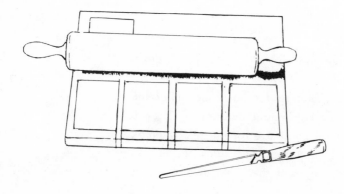

Step 4: Allow the slabs to firm up sufficiently for easy handling. Attach the walls to the base by scoring the base around the edges and scoring each wall where it will be attached to the base and where it will join another wall.

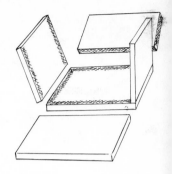

Step 5: Press the walls firmly to the base and to each other. Make a small thin coil and place it inside the box where the walls join the base. Make four more tiny coils and place them along the wall at each corner angle. Work the coils into the clay with a modeling tool and blend with your fingers where necessary.

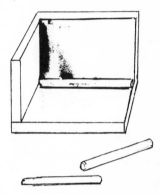

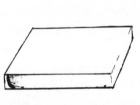

Step 6: Smooth any unevenness with a damp sponge. Make sure the joints are secure. Smooth over any sharp edges or corners. If you wish to texture the box, this may be done now. The slabs may also be textured before the box is put together.

Step 7: A slab lid will fit better if it has a flange. To make a flange on the lid, cut small slab strips and attach them to the underside so that the flange rests inside the walls of the box. To make a foot for the box, invert the form and attach slab strips to its bottom.

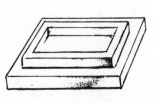

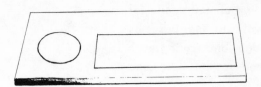

Step 8: To make a handle for the lid, use a coil, slab, or modeled form to fit the shape of the box. Attach the handle, scoring and using slip.

Step 9: Cover the box with plastic and allow it to dry thoroughly. If the box has a lid, it should be left on the form while it is drying and when it is bisque-fired to assure proper fit and keep warping to a minimum. In all lidded pieces (slab or other construction), the area where the lid and the basic form touch should be left unglazed. Otherwise the glaze will fuse the two pieces when they are fired.

Step 10: Fire and glaze.

Note: Variations on the box may be used to form a great variety of unlidded rectangular slab forms.

The same procedure may also be used to form a round box. In this case, cut a round base and lid. Instead of cutting four rectangular slabs for the body of the box, cut one long slab, measured to fit around the base. Curve it into a cylinder, score the seam, and join using slip. Proceed as for a square box.

FREE-FORM CONSTRUCTIONS

The slab work described so far has been made from carefully rolled-out slabs of uniform construction, measured exactly, to form precise geometric shapes. It is advisable for beginners to familiarize themselves with these techniques so they are able to apply them in making basic forms of this nature. Once the technique has been mastered, it is pos-

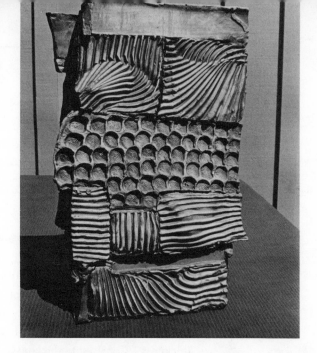

Free form multi-slab weed pot employing a variety of textures. The slabs used for construction of this piece vary in size, and to some degree, in thickness. Some are completely flat; some are very slightly curved. Made by Michi Zimmerman. (Photograph by Howard M. Berliant)

sible to depart, often radically, from this exact type of construction and evolve free forms made from slabs of varying shapes, textures, and even somewhat different thickness.

In making a free construction of this type, you may begin with a basic design in mind and allow the form to evolve as you are building it. As in all other slab constructions, the clay must be well-wedged, the slabs firm enough to handle, and each slab properly scored and attached with slip and blended into the other with a modeling tool and/or your fingers. If the piece is to be taller than 6 or 8 inches, allow it to firm up sufficiently between additions (as in coil pottery) so that the drier clay will support the weight of the addition. Don't try to build an 18-inch slab pot at one work session, since

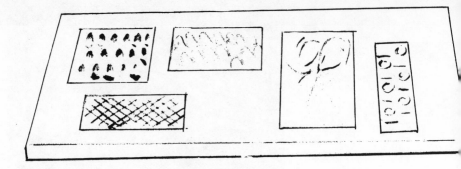

the weight of the clay will likely cause the collapse of the entire piece.

For making free-form constructions, the clay may be rolled out with a rolling pin, flattened by hand, or sliced from a block of clay with a cutting wire—in each case making slabs of more or less uniform thickness. Consistent thickness, while advisable in any clay construction, is not as essential here as in making a box, where each side must match exactly to integrate the finished piece into a unified whole. Here the slabs may vary slightly in thickness. Some may be curved a bit while others may be completely straight, depending on whether the form is to be basically rectangular or cylindrical. This is an excellent project in which to use a variety of textures to unify the piece and contribute design to its surface.

MATERIALS

Cutting wire (if you plan to cut slabs from a clay block)

Rolling pin and guide sticks (if you plan to roll out the slabs)

Sharp knife

Pencil or sharp tool for scoring

Thin sheet of plastic or plastic bag

Step 1: Roll, slice or pound enough wedged clay into one or more slabs of the proper size for the piece you will be making. If the piece will be ex-

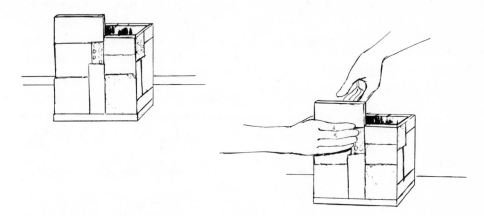

ceptionally large, prepare only enough clay to make slabs for your initial work sessions. Repeat process for additional sections of the pot.

Step 2: With a sharp knife, cut the rolled-out clay into slabs of the desired size and shape. Texture the clay in a variety of ways, using some of the ideas you developed in Chapter 5. (The pot may also be textured after it is completed.)

Step 3: Allow the slabs to firm up sufficiently so they may be handled without damage. If the slabs are to be very flat, you may want to score the backs to reduce warping.

Step 4: Score the base and slabs to be attached to it. Using slip, join the initial slabs to the base. Add slabs to each other, scoring and using slip as you go. Score and blend the slabs into each other mainly from the inside of the piece, so as not to disturb the textures on the outside. Be sure that each slab is welded firmly onto the one adjoining it. You may use small clay coils at the junctures on the inside of the piece to give added support.

Step 5: If the piece is to be large, allow it to firm up for several hours after building to a height of 6 to 8 inches until the desired height is reached. (No more than two or three additions are recommended for initial constructions.)

Step 6: When the entire form is completed, cover it with plastic and let it dry slowly. Since many slabs of slightly varying thicknesses have been joined, slow drying is essential to minimize cracking and warping. If cracks develop before the piece is dry, score and use slip to fuse them. If slight cracks develop after the piece is dry, they should not significantly undermine the design of the piece. Since this is a free construction, slight cracks might even add to the design.

Step 7: Allow the form to dry completely. Fire and glaze.

DOWEL ROD TECHNIQUE

While the previous projects have employed the standard technique of flattening a slab of clay with a rolling pin (or slicing slabs from a block or pounding them flat by hand), there is another lesser-known technique that may be used to form slab pots. This employs the use of a dowel or broom handle or rolling pin in the formation of larger pieces. For lack of a better phrase, this will be referred to as the "dowel rod technique." It involves making a large coil, inserting a dowel directly through the center, and rolling the clay on a table or other work surface much as in making a flat slab. The difference here is that the dowel is placed inside the clay, rather than used on its surface, and that the slab is formed into a cylinder around the dowel, rather than being rolled out into a flat slab that is then joined.

With a little practice, the dowel rod technique provides a unique method for quickly making seam-free cylinders and variations thereof. Clay used for this type of construction should be well-wedged, plastic, and firm enough so that it does not sag when the form is turned upright. The thickness of

This dowel-rod made pot has been incised and expanded. Its shape has been somewhat distorted from the original shape it had when constructed by the dowel-rod technique. Made by Clayton Bailey in 1964. *(Photograph courtesy of the artist)*

the walls (½- to ¾-inch thick) will add to the form's stability. The clay should not be too dry or it will be likely to crack when the rod is inserted or the form is rolled. A little experimentation will enable you to judge accurately the proper wetness of the clay.

Step 1: Form a piece of wedged clay into a thick coil.

Step 2: Insert a wooden dowel stick about ½ inch in diameter directly through the center of the coil lengthwise.

Step 3: Roll the clay-enclosed dowel on your work surface in a continuous even back-and-forth motion, much as you would when rolling out a flat slab with a rolling pin. Be sure that all surfaces of the clay come into contact with the work surface evenly. The

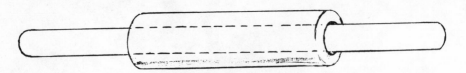

pressure of the dowel on the inside of the clay and the table on the outside causes the coil to expand into a tube. As you continue rolling, the tube continues to expand into a cylinder.

Step 4: If further opening is desired, carefully remove the dowel as soon as the clay begins to sag (this happens when the clay form becomes significantly wider than its inside support), and immediately insert a wider dowel or broom handle into the opening. Continue rolling as above, using even pressure and exposing all areas equally to the surface of the table on which you are working. When the form is finished, the walls should be about ½- to ¾-inch thick. This is a bit thicker than many constructions, but for this technique some thickness is required to keep the pot from collapsing. To make a still wider opening, a rolling pin or other thick dowel may be inserted into the cylinder by the same method.

Step 5: Cut a flat round slab to fit approximately the outside circumference of the cylinder and place it on a bat. This will be the bottom of the dowel construction. (Exact fit is not necessary at this time, since the base may be trimmed to size later.) You may also prepare the base in advance (that is, before rolling out the cylinder), keeping in mind the approximate size of the finished cylinder and cutting the base somewhat larger than you believe the opening will be. Again the base may be trimmed after the cylinder is inverted upon it and the form has dried slightly.

Step 6: Using the dowel or broom handle to support the piece from the inside, invert the horizontal form to an upright position upon the prepared base.

Footed piece with low fire matt glaze. This piece was made using the dowel-rod technique. A tapered dowel rather than one of uniform size was used to give the conical shape to each section of the piece. This 15-inch-high form was made by Clayton Bailey in 1962. (Photograph courtesy of the artist)

Your fingers should not have to touch the form at all. You now have a slab pot with no seams and no finger marks.

Step 7: Allow the form to rest on the base until it has firmed up sufficiently to be handled gently. Trim the base to fit the dowel construction. Score the area at the juncture of base and main form. Use a little slip and work the cylinder into the base, welding the parts together securely. Texture as desired.

Step 8: Allow the pot to dry thoroughly. Fire and glaze.

Notes: Variations on the cylindrical form are of course possible after the initial shaping is completed. As one example, a short wide cylinder, attached to a base, may be pushed out at the side with your hands to become a bowl.

A tapered dowel, rather than one all the same width, may be used to create forms that are conical rather than cylindrical in shape.

Just as the base was added from a rolled-out slab, a top piece may be added, using slab or other techniques such as pinching or coiling, to vary the treatment of the rim and function of the form.

10

DO-IT-YOURSELF MOLDS

There are many ways to use molds in making pottery. Most conventionally molded forms are made with the aid of plaster molds—used either for slip casting or as press, drape, or hump molds. Plaster molds are used extensively in commercial potteries where it is necessary to copy the same form perhaps thousands of times.

One of the great joys in creating pottery by hand is that each piece is a unique creation. It is generally not the ambition of the home potter to turn out row upon row of exact clay duplications. However, molds do enable the potter to create forms that are not as easily produced in other ways and to repeat a form over and over again. While this process may yield interesting finished products, it involves time and work in creating the initial form, making the mold, and casting each piece. If this technique is of special interest to you, there are many books that describe it in great detail.

There are so many interesting possibilities to explore without the use of plaster molds that this author feels that the beginner can best invest his time and imagination in other ways. If you wish to experiment with a mold of some sort, you can use household articles to make simple "do-it-yourself" molds.

Clay can be wrapped, coiled, curved, modeled, or draped inside of or over a great variety of forms. Paper-towel tubes or toilet-paper rolls provide excellent possibilities for making slab vases, bottles, or candlesticks. Oatmeal or milk cartons serve as a base for larger constructions—coiled or slab. Mixing bowls form a mold for hanging planters or other bowls. Crumpled newspaper can give a modeled or slab mask three dimensional appeal or can be used to stuff a hanging slab pot. Glass bottles can be used as molds for ceramic bottles or vases. These are only a few suggestions. Many more come to mind almost immediately . . . use a plate as a mold to make another plate, a large ball to contour a single slab dish (by draping the slab over the ball), and so on. As you work in this area, you will arrive at many original ideas of your own.

A form used for a mold should be simple in design. If you plan to shape the clay on the outside of a rigid form, such as a glass bottle, the clay construction must be removed as soon as it is firm enough to hold its shape. Otherwise the clay will crack as it shrinks against the resistant mold. Strips of paper towel placed over the mold facilitate easy removal of the clay form. If you were to shape the clay directly over (or inside of) the form, the clay would stick to the mold. Flexible molds like paper towel tubes may be left in the construction until the clay is somewhat firmer since they will "give" a bit as the clay dries. Crumpled newspaper does not have to be removed at all, since it will fire out in the first firing.

USING NEWSPAPERS

Hanging Weed Pot

MATERIALS
Guide sticks
Rolling pin
Pattern
Sharp knife
Newspaper
Wooden board or large bat

A hanging weed pot may be made from soft clay slabs stuffed with newspaper. Since this piece is made to hang against a wall, be sure that the back is kept flat while the front bellies sufficiently to hold the contents to be displayed. Make the piece large

Hanging weed pot made over
crumpled newspaper.
Donna Oestreich.
(Photograph by Howard M. Berliant)

enough to show up well in the area in which you
plan to use it.

Step 1: Make a pattern for the piece. Two pattern pieces will probably be sufficient, one for the
front of the piece, one for the back. Since the top
slab will be curved by the newspaper, you may
want to make it a bit larger than the bottom slab.

Step 2: Roll out a sufficient amount of clay on
your work surface. One way to provide instant texture is to roll the clay on burlap.

Step 3: Place the pattern pieces on the slab and
cut around them with a sharp knife.

Step 4: Allow the slabs to firm up only until they
may be handled gently without damage. Carefully
lift the bottom slab and place it on a board, large
bat, etc., where it will be allowed to dry to the
leather-hard stage without being moved.

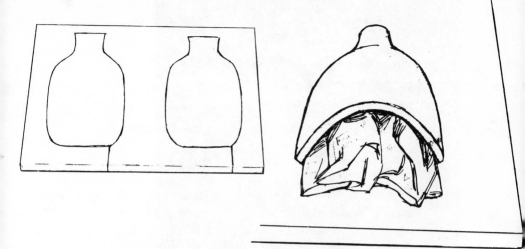

Step 5: Crumple sheets of newspaper until they form a wad somewhat smaller than the clay slabs that will enclose the paper. Place the crumpled paper over the bottom slab. Carefully lift the top slab and place it over the bottom one. You now have two clay slabs, one on top of the other with a padding of newspaper between them.

Step 6: Pinch the edges of the slabs together firmly on all sides except the top, enclosing the newspaper within the form. The clay should be soft enough so that scoring is not necessary. (If you prefer not to have a "pinch" texture around the edges, allow the slabs to stiffen. Score and use slip.) The newspaper acts as padding to contour the upper slab.

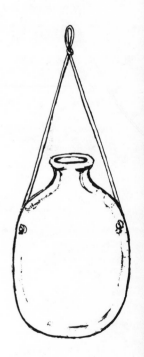

Step 7: Cover the piece with plastic and allow it to dry slowly to the leather-hard stage. Trim any uneven edges with a sharp knife. Smooth with a damp sponge. If the piece has a wide neck, the newspaper may be left inside. It will disintegrate in the kiln when the piece is fired. Make a hole (or holes) on each side of the weed pot so that it may be hung.

Step 8: Allow the piece to dry completely. Fire and glaze.

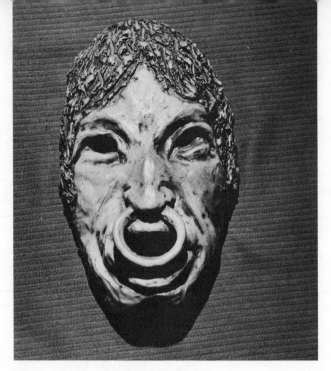

Mask made over crumpled newspaper. Student work. (Photograph by Howard M. Berliant)

Three-dimensional Mask

MATERIALS
Same as for hanging weed pot

Step 1: Roll out the clay with a rolling pin. Using a pattern if you wish, cut the shape of the mask from the rolled-out slab with a sharp knife. When the slab has firmed slightly, you may cut out the features and/or add modeled features from additional bits of clay. (Features may also be added when the piece is leather-hard rather than at this stage. If you choose to add them later, merely cut out the basic mask form and proceed as follows.)

Step 2: Crumple a sufficient amount of newspaper to make a wad somewhat smaller than the size of your mask and about two or three inches thick. Place the crumpled paper on a board, etc., where the mask may be left undisturbed until it is leather-hard.

Step 3: Carefully lift the mask onto the crumpled paper. Gently pat it around the paper until it assumes the contours you wish it to have.

Step 4: Allow the mask to dry on the newspaper padding until it is leather-hard. Trim off any excess clay from the edges. Smooth with a damp sponge where needed. If you wish to use the mask as a hanging piece, punch two holes at the top or at the sides so that it may be suspended from a cord or attached directly to a wall.

Step 5: If you have not added features in Step 1 either by cutting or modeling, do so now. At this stage, it is necessary to score the piece and the additions at the points where they will be joined and to use slip to attach any parts. Blend the features into the face with your fingers. You may add modeled eyebrows, lips, nose, small coils for hair or eyelashes, textured decorative designs with a tool, and so on.

Step 6: Allow the mask to dry thoroughly. Lift it carefully off the newspaper. It is all right if a bit of paper sticks to the underside; this will fire out in the kiln. Fire and glaze.

Note: In decorating a mask, you may want to use bright engobes, when the clay is leather-hard to give the piece some of the vivid colors characteristic of many tribal ceremonial masks.

USING PAPER TUBES

MATERIALS
Guide sticks
Rolling pin
Sharp knife
Paper towel tube or toilet paper roll

A paper tube may be used as a mold for a slab vase, employing one of several different methods to construct the piece. You may enclose the tube with one slab of clay, pinching or scoring the edges to make one seam. The tube may be cased by two slabs and pinched or scored at each end to make two seams. Or many slabs may be blended together to make a multislab construction. The basic directions given here, for a one-seam vase, bottle, or other such object may be varied according to your individual taste.

Step 1: Roll the clay into a slab. Consider the height and width of the paper tube. The slab must be long enough and wide enough to fit around the tube.

Step 2: Lay the tube on the rolled-out clay and cut a rectangle a bit longer than the tube and at least wide enough to fit around it. If you wish to pinch the seam, make the slab a little wider than the tube so that enough clay remains for pinching. If you plan to score the sides, make the slab wide enough to fit loosely around the tube. Cut a circle for the base somewhat larger than the opening in the tube, allowing for the width of the clay slab. The base circle should be about ½-inch wider in diam-

Hinged, lidded bottle by Anni Grundler. This form was made by wrapping textured clay around a paper towel tube. *(Photograph by Howard M. Berliant)*

eter than the tube opening if the slab is ½-inch thick.

Step 3: Wrap the tube with two or three layers of newspaper or paper toweling, covering the length of the tube and the end that is to be the base of the pot. Lay the tube at one end of the rectangle, wrap the clay around it, and pinch the ends together in a seam. If you wish to score the edges instead, allow the clay to firm up a bit before joining. Since the slab will be curved strongly, do not wait too long. Use slip in the scored areas. Smooth the seam with your fingers.

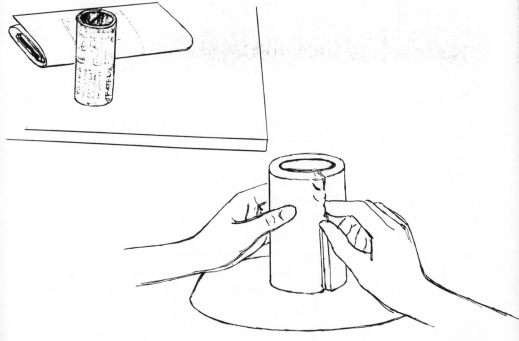

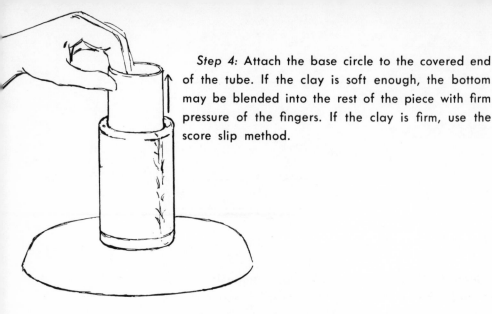

Step 4: Attach the base circle to the covered end of the tube. If the clay is soft enough, the bottom may be blended into the rest of the piece with firm pressure of the fingers. If the clay is firm, use the score slip method.

Step 5: After the clay is dry enough to hold its shape easily, carefully pull the tube out of the form, leaving the newspaper in to stabilize the form. The newspaper will fire out in the kiln. Trim away any excess clay. Allow the piece to dry thoroughly. Fire and glaze.

USING OATMEAL BOXES

Other paper forms such as oatmeal boxes, salt containers, or milk cartons may be used in much the same way as paper tubes. They may serve as molds for slab or coil constructions.

Step 1: Cover the box completely with newspaper.

Step 2: Cut the slab as in the previous project and wrap it around the box. To cover an oatmeal box, one or more slabs may be used. In encasing a milk carton, it is best to cut four rectangles of appropriate size and join them at each seam, either by pinching or scoring. Attach the base as in the previous project.

Step 3: Since these boxes are more rigid than paper tubes (which tend to soften slightly under the influence of wet clay), remove them from the inside of the clay construction as soon as the clay has firmed sufficiently to hold its shape without collapsing. Otherwise they may offer enough resistance to the drying form for cracks to develop. The newspaper may be left in the form since it will disintegrate in the firing process.

Step 4: Allow the form to dry slowly. Smooth any uneven edges if necessary when the pot is leather-hard.

Step 5: Let the piece dry thoroughly. Fire and glaze.

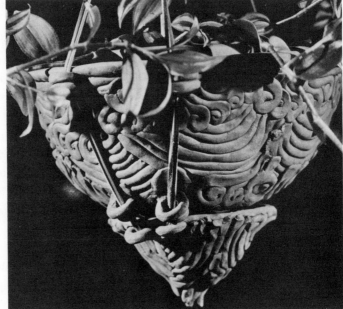

Coiled hanging planter in two sections. The two parts are strung together with leather thongs. Made by Diana Bohn. *(Photograph by Howard M. Berliant)*

USING MIXING BOWLS

Coiled Bowls or Hanging Planter

MATERIALS
Mixing bowl
Rubber kidney
Paper towel strips
Sheet of thin plastic or plastic bag

It is possible to use coils as well as slabs to form pieces inside or over another form. Coils may be placed in designs around the aforementioned oatmeal box or salt container. At times it may be necessary to attach these to the form with pins to hold a particular shape. They may be placed loosely around a paper tube to form a symmetrical coil bottle. Or they can be laid in designs inside a bowl to make textured planters or other coiled bowls.

Any simple bowl may be used as a mold for a coiled bowl; a plastic or metal mixing bowl or another ceramic bowl will work well if lined with strips of paper toweling. You may want to make several small bowls for your first project, varying the designs in each to see which pleases you most before embarking on a larger construction.

Step 1: From moist plastic clay, roll as many coils as you think you will need for your bowl. Cover them with plastic to keep them from drying out.

Step 2: Line the mold bowl with strips of paper towel. In this case, paper towel strips are used rather than a sheet of newspaper since the small strips follow the contour of the bowl more closely and keep the clay from wrinkling. Starting at the bottom, shape the coils into any desired design, covering the bottom of the bowl completely. Blend the coils into each other firmly with your fingers, working the clay from the coils into the spaces between them.

Step 3: Add coils, continuing your design up the sides of the bowl, blending each successive coil into the adjacent ones. Continue in this manner until the inside of the bowl is completely covered with coils. For this project, it is especially important to work the coils into each other well on the inside of the piece—since this is the only joining process used. If the coils are not sufficiently blended, the pot may come apart at the junctures.

Step 4: If you wish to eliminate finger marks (not necessary for a planter, but advisable for a bowl) use a rubber kidney to smooth the inside of the form.

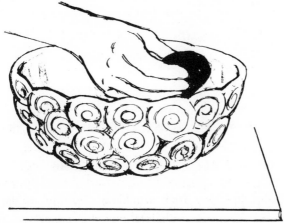

Step 5: Allow the bowl to dry to the leather-hard stage. Since the clay is placed inside rather than over a mold, shrinkage will only cause it to come away from the sides of the bowl, so it is not in any imminent danger of cracking.

Step 6: For a planter, punch two to four holes along the upper edges of the bowl so it may be hung.

Step 7: Remove the piece from the bowl mold. The coils should have remained intact on the outside of the piece and the bowl should be the same shape as the model bowl.

Step 8: Allow the piece to dry completely. Fire and glaze.

Clay bottles by Michi Zimmerman. These bottles were made from several textured slabs. Glass bottles were used as molds. (Photograph by Howard M. Berliant)

USING BOTTLES

MATERIALS
Simple-shaped bottle to use as a mold
Paper towels
Sheet of plastic or plastic bag

By now it should be evident that almost any simple shape may serve as a mold for clay construction. So far we have discussed molds that were either completely even in shape (paper towel tubes, oatmeal boxes) or that were open (bowls). However, simple narrowed forms, such as bottles, may also be used as molds, keeping in mind one variation in construction. When building around a paper towel tube, the form is made the same width at the neck as at the base. Therefore, the whole piece can be built around the mold and the mold pulled out from the top at the appropriate stage. If a narrow-necked bottle is used for the mold and the bottle is totally enclosed, it is impossible to pull the bottle, with its wider base, out through the narrow neck opening. When making a piece of this nature, the bottle is encased in clay along its sides and top but not at the base. When the clay is sufficiently firm, the bottle is pulled out from the bottom and a base is added after it has been removed.

When you are modeling clay around a bottle or other completely rigid form, the bottle must be covered with paper or cloth. It is best to fit the clay around it as loosely as possible to allow for slight shrinkage. It is also essential to remove the clay as soon as possible since the bottle will not "give" at all. If the drying clay encounters the rigid resistance of the bottle, the piece will crack.

Since bottles do not have the completely simple shapes of the forms we have discussed up to now, it is generally not advisable to use only one or two slabs for making a piece of this nature. Many small slabs placed next to each other and welded together will follow the contours of the bottle mold much more effectively than a few large ones.

Step 1: Select a simple bottle shape. Cover its sides completely with pieces of paper toweling.

Step 2: Roll, slice, or pound a sufficient number of slabs to cover the bottle. (Since the slabs will be braced by the bottle, a form made in this way may be made taller in one work session than a pot where the clay must completely support itself.) Cut a slab somewhat larger than the base of the bottle to use as its bottom.

Step 3: Beginning at the bottom sides of the bottle, form slabs around the bottle, joining one slab to another by scoring and using slip. Since you will not be able to blend all the slabs from the inside even when the bottle is removed, be sure to attach each to the other firmly on the outside. Continue adding slabs, scoring, and using slip until the bottle is covered. Finger and modeling-tool marks may be left as part of the texture or be removed with a rubber kidney, wooden rib, trimming tool, or other such object before the pot is leather-hard.

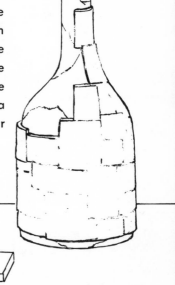

Step 4: Cover the bottle with a thin sheet of plastic and allow it to dry slowly just until the clay is stiff enough to hold its shape. Gently slide the bottle out from the clay form.

Step 5: Check the clay bottle for any cracks. If you discover some, patch them, scoring and using slip. Cover the bottle with plastic and allow it to dry slowly until it is almost leather-hard. Trim the edges of the bottle to make a straight bottom wall.

Step 6: Score the bottom edges of the bottle. Score the base where it will be attached. Press the bottom to the bottle shape firmly. Score the outside at the juncture of the bottle and base. Work a little slip into this area. Blend with a modeling tool and your fingers. Smooth any rough areas with a damp sponge.

Step 7: Cover the bottle with plastic and allow it to dry completely. Fire and glaze.

Note: Since the slabs are not blended into each other on the inside of the piece, the form may not be completely watertight. Small spaces or cracks may occur at the junctures. Therefore, these bottles are best used as purely decorative forms or weed containers and should not be used for holding liquids.

All projects and techniques discussed heretofore have used pottery clay that must be fired at the high temperatures of a ceramic kiln in order to create durable permanent products. These forms are then glazed and refired in the kiln. The glaze-firing achieves two purposes: to add color, finish, and design to the piece; and to ensure that it will be watertight. The use of ceramic clays, glazes, and kiln-firing are recommended for all aspects of pottery.

There may be some occasions, however, when you wish to work with clay and do not have a kiln at your disposal. At such times you may want to try some of the available claylike compounds that do not require kiln-firing or glazing. There are several products on the market that can be air-dried or oven-baked to permanent hardness. After they have dried completely, they may be painted with acrylic, latex, tempera, or any water-base paints.

The modeling compounds described above are packaged under various brand names—Sculpey, Polyform, Polycraft, Elasticlay, Marble-X, Mexican Pottery Clay, to name a few. They come in two basic variations—those that need only air-drying, or are self-hardening, and those which must be baked in an oven to become permanently hard. They are packaged in moist form and stay pliable when kept in a plastic bag in a container. While some of these products are initially rather stiff, they become more easily workable as they are kneaded.

Unlike ceramic clays, non-fire clays do not shrink or shrink only minimally when drying. Therefore, the finished product will be much the same size when completed and dried as when initially formed. These compounds vary in hardness, from those that nearly resemble fired ware to those that are still pliable after baking. Each is particularly suited for a specific purpose—the ones that become permanently hard for non-fire pottery constructions on

11

NON-FIRE CLAYS

a small scale, the ones that remain somewhat pliable for toys or other objects where handling is required. While many of these clays may be molded, one particular type is especially designed for this purpose. They can be purchased in quantities from 20 ounces to 25 pounds. Specific directions for the use of each product are included on the package. Be sure to read these instructions carefully as each brand has its own slight variations. Some companies will also provide, upon request, further information, project advice, and newsletters.

These products are nontoxic and ready to use, making them excellent transitional materials to introduce children to modeling permanent forms. They can provide some of the same simple experiences as "regular" clay while allowing the child to produce durable forms without the frustration of the long waiting period that is sometimes involved when a piece must first dry, be bisqued, be glazed, and then be refired (especially true if you do not have your own kiln and cannot fire at will). Here the child must wait only for the piece to dry before painting it. Another advantage of using non-fire clays with children is that they are able to see the colors used in decorating as they apply them. This is not true with glazes, where the raw glaze rarely resembles the fired color. It is sometimes difficult to convey to a small child that the gray "paint" he is using to glaze a pot will actually be green, blue, or brown. Since these pieces are painted, the colors are often brighter than kiln-fired ware. Even the novice can achieve designs that stay exactly as they were when painted on.

OVEN-FIRE PRODUCTS

The foregoing comments are generally applicable for non-firing clays. However, there are a few specific additions to be made for the oven-firing varieties.

Oven-firing clays may be reused until the time they are fired. Baking changes them to permanent products that cannot be re-formed and used again. However, if you are not satisfied with your form after baking, some changes may still be made. If a piece is found to be too small or lacking in detail, additional parts may be added onto the baked product and the entire form rebaked. The longer the piece remains in the oven, the harder and darker it gets. Fifteen to thirty minutes in a 300° to 325° F. oven is the recommended baking time.

Because of these clays' low firing temperature, hooks, pins, and hangers may be put into the finished piece before heating without danger of melting and will remain permanently embedded after the piece has been baked. In this way, one can make a pin without having to glue on the findings after it is fired. Simply form, insert pin on the back, bake, and paint. All projects must be baked before painting.

These clays may also be carved, sanded, or drilled after baking. They should not crack, break, craze, or chip under ordinary usage. If a piece does come apart in the oven (or at a later date) it can be successfully mended with white glue. Oven-firing clays may be fashioned over wire or other suitable armatures. They are waterproof, provided that the paint used on them is also waterproof. Therefore, they may be used for such objects as vases and garden containers but are not suitable for cooking or eating ware because the paint will not stand repeated moisture and will lift off.

Steps in Using Oven-Fire Clays

Step 1: Knead the clay until it becomes soft.

Step 2: Shape it into the desired form, using modeling as a technique, or applying one of the other methods discussed in the previous chapters. (These products are recommended for making small projects.)

Step 3: Place the finished form on a cookie sheet and bake fiteen to thirty minutes in a preheated 300° to 325° F. oven.

Step 4: Cool. Paint with water-base paint. If you wish, use shellac or transparent plastic spray coating for a glossy waterproof finish.

SELF-HARDENING PRODUCTS

Self-hardening clays that need only air drying to become permanently hard resemble oven-fire products in many ways. However they are not waterproof, so they may be used only in making pieces that will not come into contact with fluids. While oven-fire clays may be reused until they are baked, air-drying clays cannot be resoftened once they dry to hardness. One formula dries to a rich red color similar to Mexican and Indian pottery. Because of its pleasing appearance as is, it needs little or no decoration and retains a true "clay" character and appearance. Another product dries light gray and may be painted with moist or dry tempera paints. Both may be treated with a glossy protective transparent finish manufactured by the company that makes the clay or coated with the other materials suggested previously.

The advantages of using self-hardening clays is that here the process of creation is all that is necessary to achieve the finished product. Simply shape and dry, and your piece is complete. No firing or baking of any kind is required. These clays may also be used for throwing small forms on the potter's wheel.

The modeling compounds above are recommended for instances when it is not feasible to use regular clays, as an experiment with a similar yet different medium, for making jewelry or other small decorative pieces, as initial ventures into permanent forms when teaching children, and when a kiln is not available. If, for example, you are planning a two-week trip to the mountains and wish to continue working with clay, these products will allow you to do so with minimal equipment (a two-pound box of modeling compound, some toothpicks for adding texture, and a small box of paints) and without worrying whether your fragile greenware will have time to dry or will withstand the trip intact. Projects recommended for these types of clays include beads, jewelry of all kinds, buttons, small modeled forms, and scaled-down versions of other projects discussed in this book. As an auxiliary experience these products provide a simple, pleasant departure from conventional pottery-making.

COOKIE-CUTTER CHRISTMAS TREE ORNAMENTS

MATERIALS
Oven-fire or air-dry clay
Cookie-cutters
Toothpicks
Ornament hooks
Water-base paints
Shellac or transparent plastic spray (optional)

Step 1: Knead the clay until it becomes pliable and easy to work with.

Step 2: Using a rolling pin, roll the clay out as for cookie dough, making it about 1/16- to 1/8-inch thick.

Step 3: Cut out the desired shapes with appropriate Christmas cookie-cutters.

Step 4: Texture or add details with a toothpick if you wish. Poke a hole at the top of the ornament

Cookie-cutter Christmas tree ornaments. These decorations were made from non-fire self-hardening clay. They were painted with tempera paints and coated with one application of shellac. By the author. (*Photograph by Howard M. Berliant*)

so that it may be hung from a string, or insert an ornament hook into the hole.

Step 5: If the clay is self-hardening, allow it to dry thoroughly. If the clay is oven-firing, place the ornaments on a cookie sheet and bake them 15 to 30 minutes at a 300° to 325° F. oven. Cool.

Step 6: Paint with your choice of colors. If you wish, coat with shellac, plastic spray, or any glossy protective finish after the paint has dried.

The techniques discussed in the previous chapters have been methods that basically involve only the clay and your hands. While some simple tools may have been used for constructing and refining pieces, with the exception of simple molds no extraneous aids were used in shaping the clay form itself.

The experiences you have had in hand-building have provided you with many attractive and functional pieces in a variety of shapes and also have given you different experiences in familiarizing yourself with clay and its many possibilities and limitations. Now that you are truly aware of the nature of the medium, you can apply this knowledge to another and in many ways different technique of forming clay.

12

THE POTTER'S WHEEL

GENERAL INFORMATION

The potter's wheel is a device for shaping completely round symmetrical forms. Round shapes can be successfully made by slab-building, coiling, or pinching, but they rarely attain the total symmetry of a wheel-thrown pot. Pottery thrown on the wheel is always round. You cannot throw a square or triangular piece. However, finished round pots may be pushed, paddled, or otherwise distorted to take on another appearance.

The potter's wheel was developed early in man's civilization. It was one of the first machines he invented. We know that the ancient Sumerians used it over 5,000 years ago, and Egyptian paintings and records tell us that it probably existed there as long ago as 6,000 years. It may have been developed simultaneously by many cultures. Early Chinese pottery pieces indicate that they were made on the wheel. The ancient Greeks used the potter's wheel as well. Whether these discoveries arose independently in each culture with the discovery of the wheel or whether they were transmitted by one culture to another is a question on which anthropologists differ even today.

Although the potter's wheel has undergone some changes since its invention the general principles involved in its use are still the same. Today there are two basic types of wheels in use: the kick wheel and the electric wheel. Although each model has several variations in construction, the speed of the former is controlled by the potter's feet, while the latter is powered by an electric motor.

The kick wheel is the direct descendant of the earliest wheel made by man. Here the potter's feet are used to kick the fly wheel (the large wheel on the bottom that causes the wheel-head to turn), while his hands shape the clay on the wheel-head. Since the speed of this type of wheel is totally controlled by the individual, it can be regulated from very slow to very fast with all nuances in between, giving the potter complete control over speed while forming a clay piece.

Because an electric wheel is powered by a motor, it frees the potter from the physical exertion of kicking the wheel—sometimes a tiring task when he is working with a large piece of clay. While the electric wheel has the advantage of conserving all one's energies for use in the building of a pot,

Kick wheel, made by Robert Brent Potter's Wheels, Santa Monica, California. This wheel can be set to go in either direction—for kicking with the right or left foot, in a clockwise or counterclockwise direction. An optional motor attachment may be purchased to allow it to be used as an electric wheel. (Photograph courtesy Robert Brent Potter's Wheels)

its slight disadvantage is that the control achieved over the speed of the wheel is not as accurate and refined as that of the kick wheel. Some wheels may be purchased as kick wheels with an optional motor attachment.

After you have worked on the wheel for some time and tried several different sorts, you will develop your own preferences for the type best suited to your needs. The same pieces can be formed on a kick and an electric wheel. While each has its particular advantages, this author recommends that initial wheel experiences should, if possible, be undertaken on a kick wheel. This is something like learning to drive a car. If you learn on a standard shift model, it is easy to drive any car. If you have only driven an automatic, you may encounter some initial difficulty learning to shift.

There are some things to bear in mind when using a potter's wheel if you are left-handed. Instructions for most wheels are geared to the right-handed person. The right-handed person works on the right side of the wheel and uses his right foot to kick the wheel in a counterclockwise direction. Some electric wheels only go counterclockwise.

The left-handed person will initially often want to work the opposite way—that is, on the left side of the wheel, kicking clockwise with his left foot. Some electric wheels can be rotated clockwise, but some cannot. Keeping these points in mind, you may find it simpler in the long run, even if you are normally left-handed, to adjust yourself to right-handed throwing. This is especially true for people who are not left-footed. If you are left-handed, experiment with these methods and choose the one that works best for you. If there is no significant difference in ease of throwing (since the process actually uses both hands about equally), you would avoid some problems if you could learn to work on the right side of the wheel and kick counterclockwise with your right foot. This would also enable you to use any sort of electric wheel.

The potter's wheel is synonymous in the minds of many people with the word pottery. By now you know that this is certainly not the only way of creating attractive ceramic pieces. However the potter's wheel does have a lure all its own. Many potters eventually become so dedicated to the wheel that almost all their pieces are made in this manner. After you have tried wheel work, you can determine how much of a part it will play in your creations. Your experiences in the realm of clay are certainly incomplete if you have never ventured into the field of throwing. While this aspect of pottery requires the learning of some basic skills and many hours of practice, it is an area well worth pursuing. It may be the most difficult technique to master in making pottery, but for many it is also the most rewarding.

To acquire the basic knowledge necessary in successfully using a potter's wheel, it is most advisable to take a class from a competent instructor at a recreation center, evening school, college, private studio, or one of the other places mentioned in previous chapters. Investigate what your community has to offer. While you may be able to learn these basic skills from a book and by lengthy experimentation on your own, there is no substitute for face-to-face instruction from a good teacher. A book can help reinforce concepts learned in a class, and experimentation will afford practice in firming up the ideas you have been taught, but watching and doing yourself under supervision are still the fastest road to success. In the following chapters, the author hopes to furnish some of the individualized instruction a busy teacher may not always be able to provide and to clear up some of the aspects of throwing that still puzzle you after class. For those who are unable to take a course at all, the author will try to teach you as simply and graphically as possible so that you can proceed on your own.

A potter's wheel is an expensive investment. It is not something to be bought on a whim because of an immediate and perhaps casual interest in this form of shaping clay. Take a class, try several different wheels, determine which best suits your needs, abilities, and pocketbook—and if the love affair persists and you become truly committed to this fascinating form of the craft, buy (or make) one of your own.

There is a certain magic involved in taking a formless lump of clay, throwing it down on the wheelhead and shaping this indistinct mass into a beautiful, symmetrical finished form. The secret of this magic lies in your own skilled fingers, which seem to make the clay come alive and do your bidding. A little pressure here, a little there, and a basic cylinder becomes a wide bowl or a narrow bottle. The speed of the potter's wheel and the pressure of your hands control the clay from the initial centering to the final shaping.

CLAY FOR THROWING

Many of the clays used in hand-building are suitable for use on the potter's wheel. All clay must be very well wedged, because air bubbles or lumps will cause your fingers to "trip" on the walls of the pot and throw the piece off center. The clay should be plastic but not overly moist since water is continually added to allow your hands to ride smoothly on its surface. If it is too wet initially, it will become soggy as you work on it and the piece will collapse. If you plan to add grog to the clay, be sure that the grog is fine-grained or it will act as an abrasive on your hands. (If you plan to work on the wheel, you must choose between the glamour of beautiful soft hands, long nails, and a good manicure, and a dedication to your craft. In throwing, more than in other techniques, you just can't have it both ways.)

TOOLS

A potter's wheel, kick or electric, is your basic tool. Other tools needed should be available in your pottery kit. These include a needle for trimming uneven rims, an elephant ear sponge for soaking up excess water, a strip of chamois leather for smoothing and finishing rims, a cutting wire if you wish to remove the form from the bat or wheel-head before it is dry. You will also need a wire trimming tool to finish the bottom of your pots after they are leather-hard. You may use a wooden rib, rubber kidney, or metal rib for adding finishing touches to bowls and other forms. A wooden modeling tool allows trimming of the wet form on the bat or wheel-head to remove excess clay. Several bats should be available so that forms may be thrown on a bat initially. If the pot is thrown directly on the wheel-head (as done by many experienced potters), there is danger for the beginner of distorting the wet piece when it is removed. If it is thrown on a bat, the whole bat may be removed from the wheel without danger of damage to the pot. A large bowl of water should always be beside you on the wheel, since the clay needs constant lubrication to keep your hands from dragging on its surface.

In previous chapters, materials were listed separately at the beginning of each project. In the following chapters they will not be listed specifically. It will be taken for granted that you have the basic tools mentioned earlier and will use the proper ones as each piece is made.

BASIC TIPS

Clay for throwing should always be formed into a ball. The rounder and more symmetrical the ball and the more it is thrown onto the direct center of the bat or wheel-head, the easier the centering of the clay will be. Begin with a ball of clay about the size of a large grapefruit. Much smaller or larger pieces are harder to handle.

The clay should always be kept moist, allowing the hands to slide over it smoothly. If your hands stick to the clay, the form will move off center.

In all steps of throwing, try to keep the clay as much on center as possible. Beginners are often impatient to center the clay and "get on with it." However, cheating—even just a little—at this or subsequent stages will show up in the pot sooner or later. A piece of clay that is not well-centered will become more and more off center at each step in its forming. So spend sufficient time to get the clay properly centered before progressing to the next stage.

The basic form in throwing is a cylinder. All other forms evolve from it. A cylinder opened out becomes a bowl. A cylinder lengthened and closed becomes a bottle. Learn to throw a well-balanced cylinder before progressing to other forms. The more time you spend learning the basics of wheel work, the more success you will have with its variations.

The walls of a thrown pot should be fairly even in thickness, although the bottom may be a bit thicker than the top to support the weight of the rest of the clay. Beginners often leave great masses of clay at the base of their pots while the rims become precariously thin. Learn to work on the pot from the bottom up—removing all excess clay from the base and bringing it rhythmically and continuously to the top. Again it must be emphasized that your initial wheel experiences will involve repetitions, attention to detail, and often frustration. You are impatient to make something to keep. But it cannot be said too strongly that the more attention you pay to getting each step of the fundamentals right, the greater your eventual success in this field will be. If you develop sloppy techniques from the beginning, it will be more difficult for you to "unlearn" these than for a newcomer to the craft to learn the correct techniques.

Don't try to keep everything. Practice your basic cylinder form and keep only those pieces that are even in thickness and symmetrical. Don't waste time trying to salvage a pot that is badly off center. Instead, rewedge the clay and start again, this time working conscientiously to keep the form on center through all stages. The best way to learn throwing is to make a cylinder according to the directions listed below and then check your work. Don't keep this cylinder even if it looks well thrown. Slice it down the middle lengthwise with your cutting wire. Check to make sure the walls are of uniform thickness, that there is no excessive clay at the bottom and bottom sides, that the rim is approximately the same thickness as the rest of the pot. Repeat the process. Do this again—ten, twenty, thirty times. If you are

Slice the cylinder down the middle and check for even wall thickness, no excessive clay at the bottom and bottom sides, rim approximately the same thickness as the rest of the pot. *(Photograph by Howard M. Berliant)*

following instructions and perfecting each step as much as possible along the way, your cylinders should show marked and progressive improvement.

Despite all cautions and repeated emphasis on executing each step conscientiously, it is still necessary to work fairly quickly when making pieces on the wheel. The longer you work the clay, the more saturated and "tired" it becomes. Once the clay is too wet and overworked, it refuses to hold its shape and begins to collapse. Work carefully, but as quickly as possible.

One last word. Do not let these cautionary remarks deter you from trying the potter's wheel. Patience, persistence, and a high frustration tolerance may be needed initially, but the results of a good grounding in the basics will pay high dividends in all your successive wheel projects.

TEN STEPS FOR THROWING

Step 1: Centering. The hands are used to push the clay exactly to the middle of the wheel.

Step 2: Opening. A hole is made in the center of the clay. The hole is widened.

Step 3: Pulling up. The clay is lifted to give the pot height and to thin the walls.

Step 4: Shaping. The pot is molded with the hands to its final form.

Step 5: Drying. The piece is allowed to dry to the leather-hard stage.

Step 6: Trimming. Excess clay is trimmed off the bottom of the pot with an appropriate tool.

Step 7: Drying. The pot is dried completely.

Step 8: Bisque-firing. The clay is fired for the first time.

Step 9: Glazing. The pot is decorated and glazed.

Step 10: Glaze-firing. The finished glazed pot is fired to maturity.

MAKING A CYLINDER

Step 1: Moisten a plaster bat. Put a little slip on the wheel-head. Place the bat on the slip and move it slightly back and forth until it is firmly anchored. In making larger pots, several wads of clay or a clay coil may be pressed against the sides of the bat for added holding power.

Step 2: Take a well-wedged ball of clay about the size of a grapefruit and "throw" it down as closely to the direct center of the bat as possible. Kick the wheel very fast (or use high speed on an electric wheel). Brace your elbows on the bar of the wheel if there is one or against the sides of your body. Try to keep your upper arms as rigid as possible. Remember that you must exert your force on the clay (that is, you must control the clay, and not vice versa).

Attach the bat to the wheelhead, using several wads of clay to anchor it firmly. *(Photograph by Howard M. Berliant)*

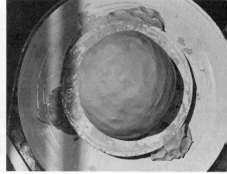

"Throw" the clay ball as closely as possible on the direct center of the bat. *(Photograph by Howard M. Berliant)*

Step 3: Moisten your hands with water. With both hands around the clay, push it toward the center of the wheel. If this is properly done, the clay will rise up in a cone.

Step 4: Cup one hand (usually your left hand if you are right-handed; opposite for lefties) around the cone and press down with the flat of your other hand. This will force the clay down again and flat-

Coning up the clay. Place both hands around the clay and push it toward the center of the wheel. If this is done properly, the clay will rise up in a cone. (Photograph by Howard M. Berliant)

Cup one hand around the clay and press down with the flat of your other hand. This will force the clay down again and flatten the cone. (Photograph by Howard M. Berliant)

A well-centered piece of clay will be smooth and symmetrical. (Photograph by Howard M. Berliant)

Push both thumbs into the center of the clay and press downward to form a well. (Photograph by Howard M. Berliant)

ten the cone. Repeat this process, coning up and pushing down again until the clay stops wobbling and hits your hands evenly when they are held around it lightly. The clay should now be smooth and symmetrical. A little practice will let you "feel" when the clay is centered. There are other ways of centering that work equally well. All aim for the result of getting the clay smooth, symmetrical, and completely in the center of the wheel. You may use any method that achieves these goals.

Step 5: Contain the revolving clay by cupping the fingers of both hands around it. Don't forget to keep kicking your wheel, or it will stop turning. You may reduce speed somewhat after the clay has been centered. Remember also to always keep the clay well-lubricated with water. Now push both thumbs into the clay and press downward to form a well. Widen the well by pressing both thumbs into it again and pulling the clay toward the edges of the hole.

Step 6: Supporting the clay with one hand (usually the left), put the fingers of the other hand into the opening and pull the clay out to widen the base. Spread the clay to the edges of the pot until the base has reached desired width. Sponge any excess water that collects on the bottom of the pot. Check the thickness of the bottom by holding your needle perpendicular to the bottom and sticking it in until it hits the bat. Approximate how far in the needle goes. The base should be ½- to ¾-inch thick, depending on the size and thickness of the piece and how much you want to recess the foot when trimming. (See section below on "Trimming.")

(Below, left) Put the fingers of one hand into the opening and pull the clay out to widen the base. Support the outside of the piece with your other hand. *(Photograph by Howard M. Berliant)*

(Below, right) Check the bottom thickness by inserting a needle through the base until it touches the bat. The base should be ½ to ¾ of an inch thick, depending upon the size of the pot and how much you wish to recess the foot when trimming. *(Photograph by Howard M. Berliant)*

Exert even pressure with both hands until a slight "ridge" develops. Pull the clay upward evenly, letting the ridge rise above your fingers as you pull. (Photograph by Howard M. Berliant)

Step 7: Now pull the clay up so that it begins to rise in a cylinder. Place one hand inside the form (use the hand that feels most comfortable for this step), fingers touching the inside wall of the pot. Place the fingers of the other hand opposite the inside hand, on the outside of the pot. Beginning at the base of the bat, exert even pressure with both hands until a slight "ridge" develops. Now pull the clay upward evenly, letting the ridge rise above your fingers as you pull. Start at the base and continue the pull in one continuous motion, lifting the clay from the bottom to the top of the cylinder. If you stop in midcylinder, you may have uneven wall thickness.

Step 8: Repeat Step 7. Each pull upward makes the form higher and thins the walls. It is important to keep your hands steady, so be sure to brace them well at all stages. Dip your hands in water often. Continue pulling up in this fashion until the cylinder has reached desired height and thinness. If the cylinder starts to flare out near the top, "collar it in" that is, cup both hands around the top

Continue pulling up until the cylinder has reached proper height and thinness. (Photograph by Howard M. Berliant)

of the pot slightly below the area where it begins to flare and push the clay gently inward by exerting pressure from the outside. Since this thickens the wall in this area, pull the excess clay up again until it is properly thin. Complete your cylinder.

To correct slight unevenness, trim the top of the pot with a needle. Press the needle against the rim of the pot, slightly below the uneven edge. As the wheel revolves the needle will cut away the excess clay. Lift off the trimmed area. (Photograph by Howard M. Berliant)

Step 9: If the top of the pot is slightly uneven, the clay has gotten off center somewhere along the way. To correct slight (but not glaring) unevenness, trim the top with a needle. Hold the edge gently between the moistened thumb and forefinger of your left hand. Spin the wheel slowly. Bracing your right hand, press the needle against the top slightly below the uneven edge. As the wheel revolves, the needle will cut away the uneven clay. Lift off the uneven part. (If the pot is badly off center do not try to correct its deficiencies. Rewedge the clay and start over.) Smooth the top of the cylinder with a damp elephant ear sponge or chamois.

Step 10: Trim excess clay from the outside of the base with a wooden tool. Remove excess clay from the bat to hasten drying and ensure easy removal of the pot. Remove the bat from the wheel-head by loosening it with a fettling knife, cutting wire, or taut string, being careful not to damage the bat.

Step 11: Allow the pot to dry to the leather-hard stage. Trim.

Trim excess clay from the outside of the base with a wooden tool. (Photograph by Howard M. Berliant)

TRIMMING

The more carefully a pot has been thrown, the less trimming it will need. While trimming can, if necessary, correct some mistakes—such as too much clay at the base—it cannot be expected to salvage a badly thrown pot. A pot is trimmed to remove excess clay, lighten it, and give it a more finished look by the addition of a foot. If you want your pot to have a recessed foot, remember to leave enough clay at the base to allow for this. The foot of the pot should always relate to the total form, as should all other areas. Before you begin trimming, look the pot over carefully. The outside of the form should harmonize with the inside. Determine in advance where and how much you should trim. Hold your trimming tool at an angle for the most efficient cutting.

Step 1: Remove the leather-hard pot from the bat. If it is sufficiently dry and the clay has been trimmed away from the bat at the edges, the pot should lift off without much trouble. If it is difficult to remove, pull a cutting wire through it at the base and sever it from the bat. (Do not remove the pot if it is too wet.)

Step 2: Turn the pot upside down on the wheelhead, placing it in what appears to be the direct center of the wheel. Brace one hand on the other. Straighten the index finger of one hand (usually the right) and place it lightly against the side of the pot. Kick the wheel gently. If your fingernail marks the pot evenly on all sides, the piece is centered. If your nail marks one section of the pot but not another (that is, leaves an incomplete ring), the form is not completely centered. Turn the wheel until the marked area is in front of you, and then push the pot gently away from you. Turn the wheel and recheck the pot with your extended finger. Adjust the form in this manner until it is evenly centered.

(Above, left) Center the pot for trimming by placing it upside down on the center of the wheelhead. Check to see that it is centered by rotating the wheel and holding an extended finger lightly against the sides of the pot. If your nail marks the pot evenly on all sides, it is centered. If the pot is marked unevenly, it needs further adjusting in centering before it is trimmed. (Photograph by Howard M. Berliant)

(Above, right) Bracing your hands against each other, press your trimming tool against the side of the pot. As the wheel revolves, the tool will cut away the excess clay. (Photograph by Howard M. Berliant)

Step 3: Now that the pot is centered, anchor it to the wheel-head with several wads of clay. Place the clay gently but firmly around the base of the form to keep it affixed to the wheel.

Step 4: Place one hand (usually the left) on top of the pot to be trimmed. Brace your right hand against the left hand by touching thumbs. Hold the trimming tool in your right hand, using mainly your thumb and first two fingers to grasp it (similar to holding chalk as opposed to holding a pencil). Press your trimming tool lightly against the bottom of the pot. Kick the wheel. As the wheel revolves, the tool will cut away the excess clay. You may trim part of the way up the pot, blending the trimmed area into the untrimmed area into a unified whole.

Step 5: To make a foot, leave a rim of clay about ½- to 1-inch wide around the bottom edge. Recess the center of the base by cutting away the clay, beginning at the middle of the base and working outward.

(Left) Recess the center of the base by cutting away the clay. Begin at the middle of the base and work outward. (Photograph by Howard M. Berliant)

(Right) The finished trimmed pot with a recessed foot. (Photograph by Howard M. Berliant)

Step 6: Smooth the trimmed area with a damp sponge. Remove the cylinder from the bat. Sponge the rim. Allow it to dry thoroughly. Fire and glaze.

The steps described for throwing a cylinder are basic in making almost any pot on the potter's wheel. The clay must always be centered, opened, and pulled up. Variations occur in the degree of pulling up and in the shaping that follows these initial steps. A bowl is formed by making a low wide cylinder and pushing the sides out rather than pulling them up. A bottle is formed by keeping the cylinder tall and slim and collaring in the top to make a narrow neck. Forms between these two extremes use aspects of both techniques. A bowl is a good project to try once you have learned to throw a cylinder because it presents fewer problems than other forms.

MAKING A BOWL

Step 1: Center a ball of clay the appropriate size for the bowl you will be making. A grapefruit-size ball is still a good amount for initial projects.

Step 2: Open the form according to general directions until the base has reached the desired width. The width of the bowl will be determined by the width that the clay is centered. For a low wide bowl the centered clay is spread into a flattened wide disc. For a tall narrow bowl the clay is centered as for a wide cylinder. Be sure to pull the clay from the middle of the base toward the outside edges so you will not have an excessive amount at the bottom of the bowl. Pull the clay up into a low cylinder. The height of the cylinder will depend on whether you are making a tall rounded bowl or a low flat one.

Step 3: After the cylinder has reached desired

Making a bowl. Support the outside of the cylinder with one hand. Place the other hand inside, opposite the outside hand, and push the wall outward. This widens the cylinder and causes it to flare out into a bowl shape. (Photograph by Howard M. Berliant)

height, support the outside of the bowl with one hand. Place the other hand inside the bowl opposite the outside hand and push the wall outward. This widens the bowl and causes it to flare out. Repeat this process until the bowl attains the desired width. The area where the clay begins to curve out from the bat should be left somewhat thicker than the rest of the bowl. If the clay is too thin here, the form will collapse. It is important to keep the curve of the bowl continuous (and for beginners) not too sharp, or again the form may collapse. The more the bowl flares, the harder it is for the clay to support itself.

Step 4: Cut any unevenness from the rim with a needle. Trim excess clay away from the bat and from the base of the bowl with a wooden tool.

Step 5: Follow procedures for drying and trimming given under the general directions.

MAKING A BOTTLE

To throw a tall vase or bottle shape, the clay is first made into a cylinder. The lower part is pushed out by pressure from the inside to form a "belly," while the top is collared in, thickened, and then pulled up and thinned to make a narrow neck.

Step 1: Follow the basic directions for making a cylinder through Step 6.

Step 2: If you plan to make your bottle "belly," leave enough clay in the bottom half of the cylinder so that the walls will not become too thin when the clay is pushed out. Place one hand inside the cylinder, fingers touching the wall. Place the fingers of your other hand opposite the inside hand, on the outside. Now push out with the inside hand as in making a bowl, supporting the clay with the outside fingers. Pull up slightly while you are pushing the clay. Continue your pull to the top of the cylinder, pulling up but not pushing out as you reach the neck. Repeat this procedure until the vase "bellies" to your taste—two to four times should be sufficient.

Step 3: Place your hands around the pot about one-third of the way from the top. Press both hands lightly against the pot to collar it in. This thickens and narrows the neck. Now pull this thickened clay up to form the neck. Repeat the process, collaring in and thickening the clay, pulling up and thinning it until you have achieved the desired shape.

Repeat collaring in and pulling up until the bottle has reached the desired shape. *(Photograph by Howard M. Berliant)*

Step 4: Trim any unevenness from the top of the bottle with a needle. Smooth the rim with a chamois or elephant ear sponge. Trim excess clay carefully away from the bottom of the bottle and from the bat, using a wooden tool.

Step 5: Remove the bat from the wheel. Allow the bottle to dry to the leather-hard stage. Trim.

TRIMMING A BOTTLE

It is most advisable to make bottles so that they require little or no extra trimming once they are removed from the wheel. Since a bottle has a long narrow neck and a wide base, it is impossible to turn the bottle upside down on the wheel-head to trim excess clay from its bottom. If you remove all

The chuck is centered on the wheelhead and fastened to it with wads of soft clay. (Photograph by Howard M. Berliant)

The bottle is centered in the chuck and attached with wads of clay or a clay coil. The bottom of the bottle may now be trimmed without injuring the neck. (Photograph by Howard M. Berliant)

superfluous clay from the base and bottom sides with a wooden tool while the bottle is still on the wheel, no further trimming should be required. If you find it necessary to trim a bottle or want to give it a recessed foot, the bottle must be set into a chuck or other hollow form. It cannot be trimmed directly on the wheel.

A chuck is a concave cylinder made of clay that has been bisque-fired. The chuck is dampened, centered on the wheel-head, and fastened to it with wads or a coil of soft clay. The bottle is placed upside down, neck inside the chuck and bottom up. The bottle is then centered in the chuck and moved around slightly and tested with your extended finger to see that it is directly on center. A clay coil anchors the bottle to the chuck. The bottom of the bottle may now be trimmed without injuring the neck.

For another way of trimming a bottle, place the chuck on the wheel-head. Level the bottle upside down in the chuck. Attach the bottle to the dampened chuck with wads of clay, then proceed to

Finished trimmed bottle. *(Photograph by Howard M. Berliant)*

center as described above, treating the bottle and chuck as one. Attach the chuck to the wheel-head with tabs of clay and trim as usual.

A chuck is easy to make. Throw some concave cylinders and bisque-fire them. Make several heights and widths for trimming different-size bottles. A plaster cylinder or even a large-mouthed glass jar or ceramic cylinder will do. The advantage of using a bisque or plaster form is that it is porous and will not slip around on the wheel when anchored by clay. Clay sticks to bisque ware or plaster more readily than to glass or fired pottery.

To make shapes intermediate between a bowl and bottle follow the basic directions for a cylinder and add modified bowl and bottle techniques to fit the shape you are making. Remember that pressure from the inside makes a form flare out. Pressure from the outside makes a pot go in. Collaring in with both hands keeps the top from flaring out. Pulling up thins the clay.

LIPS AND RIMS

The rim of the pot is often neglected by the beginning potter. But since the rim is the place where the pot ends, the eye focuses upon it immediately. The lip can provide the difference between an interesting and an ordinary pot. Often a bowl or other simple shape requires only a soft touch with a chamois or sponge to give it a smooth, simple, rounded rim. The lip of a pitcher, ash tray, casserole, or other pot of this nature is functional as well as decorative. The rim serves a definite purpose—to help the form pour, to hold a cigarette, to contain a lid, and so on. You must keep in mind the purpose of the lip as well as its design. In pottery, as in other functional crafts, form must always be tailored to use.

To make a lip, hold the clay gently between the moist thumb and forefinger of one hand while the index finger of the other hand depresses the area that is to be the lip. For an upturned rim, support the edge with both hands from underneath and turn it up slightly. Or for a thickened lip, roll the rim under. By changing the pressure of your fingers, you can create a variety of rims to complement the total design of your pot. In making a foot or a lip, always try to keep it in harmony with the rest of the pot.

(Below, left) To make a lip, hold the clay gently between the moist thumb and forefinger of one hand while the index finger of the other hand depresses the area that is to be the lip. *(Photograph by Howard M. Berliant)*

(Below, right) For a thickened lip, roll the rim under. *(Photograph by Howard M. Berliant)*

Throwing "off the hump." Center a large ball of clay. Center a small part of this clay to form a "hump" at the top of the larger piece. (Photograph by Howard M. Berliant)

THROWING "OFF THE HUMP"

Throwing "off the hump" is a technique especially suited to making small pieces. It involves centering one large ball of clay and then centering a small part of that clay on the larger centered piece and creating a small form from this hump.

Step 1: Center a large ball of clay. Center a small part of this clay to form a "hump" at the top of the larger piece.

Step 2: Form the pot out of this hump according to general throwing procedures.

Form the pot out of this hump according to general throwing procedures.
(Photograph by Howard M. Berliant)

Place a cutting wire at the base of the pot. Rotate the wheel slowly and cut the piece off the hump with the wire. *(Photograph by Howard M. Berliant)*

Step 3: When the form is completed, dry your hands thoroughly. Place a cutting wire at the base of the pot. Rotate the wheel slowly and cut the piece off the hump with the wire. Gently remove and place it on a bat to dry.

Step 4: Center another small "hump" on the clay. Repeat the procedure in Steps 2 and 3. Continue in this manner until all the clay has been used up. This method enables you to throw many small pieces without using a fresh bat each time and without having to undertake the total centering process for every pot. It is a quick way of turning out many small pieces in a short time with a minimum of effort. It is also a good technique for making a set of small matching pots such as mugs or bowls.

13

ACCOUTREMENTS TO WHEEL THROWING

Now that you know how to make a basic cylinder and are becoming more proficient in its two most extreme variations, the bowl and the bottle, you are also surely creating intermediate forms of your own design. In expanding basic shapes, you will at times want to add other parts to them to vary their form and function. You may wish to throw some small cylinders and add handles to make them into mugs. You might form a pouring lip on a tall, modified bottle shape, add a handle, and make a pitcher. A bowl with a lid becomes a casserole. A rounded form with a lid and spout turns into a teapot. Knowing how to make handles, lids, knobs, and spouts will again give you a broader base from which to work and add to the variety of experimentation you may pursue.

PULLING HANDLES

A thrown piece generally looks best with a pulled handle. Since this type of handle has a similar fluidity of line and bears the mark of the potter's fingers, it complements these same qualities in the thrown pot.

Clay used for pulling handles must be well-wedged and very plastic but somewhat stiffer than clay used for throwing. Always use plenty of water and "pull" the handle with even downward strokes —working from the top to the bottom in a rhythmic, consistent motion. Uneven jerky pulling or hard squeezing will cause the handle to become too thin in parts and break off. Pulling well-shaped even handles takes practice. Don't despair if your first efforts don't live up to your expectations. Practice will bring measurable improvement.

Handles are for holding. Always keep this paramount in your mind when considering size, shape, and width. A large pitcher will of course need a

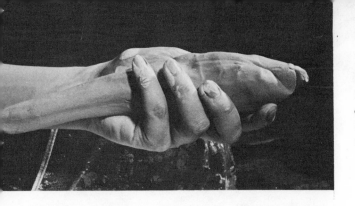

Form a piece of wedged clay into a thick tapered coil. *(Photograph by Howard M. Berliant)*

stronger handle than a small mug. When shaping a handle, also remember that it will employ both positive and negative space as part of its design— positive space in the shape of the handle itself; negative space in the empty area enclosed by the form of the handle. To pull a handle:

Step 1: Form a piece of wedged clay into a thick tapered coil.

Step 2: Hold the coil in your left hand (reverse for lefties). Wet your right hand and hold it firmly around the top part of the clay. Stroke the clay downward, holding it between your thumb and fingers and pressing slightly as you pull. This will lengthen and thin the handle. Continue stroking the clay downward, thumb on top of the handle, fingers underneath, until the handle is the desired length and thinness. Do not squeeze the clay, because this will cause the handle to break. Use your thumb to impress the handle, making an indentation in the clay characteristic of a pulled handle. The thicker part at the top becomes the top part of the handle, the thinner part the handle's bottom.

Stroke the clay downward, holding it between your thumb and fingers and pressing slightly as you pull. Use your thumb to impress the handle, making an indentation in the clay characteristic of a pulled handle. *(Photograph by Howard M. Berliant)*

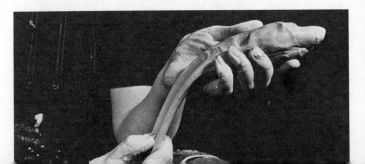

Cut the handle to approximate size. Pre[ss] the top of the handle onto a bat. Be[nd] the rest of the handle to desired sha[pe] and allow it to firm up on the bat until [it] can be attached without distorting [its] shape. *(Photograph by Howard M. Berlia[nt])*

Step 3: Cut the handle to size. Press the top of the handle onto a bat. Bend the rest of the handle into its desired shape and allow it to dry on the bat until it is firm enough to be touched without distorting its shape.

Step 4: To attach the handle to the pot, score the leather-hard, trimmed piece where the handle will be affixed, both at the top and bottom. Score handle. Apply slip to the scored surfaces. Press the top of the handle to the upper scored surface, anchoring it firmly to the pot. The area of juncture may be scored again and smoothed with a modeling tool or your fingers. For a large form such as a teapot or pitcher, a small clay coil should be placed around the juncture for added support. Blend the handle into the main form carefully. It should flow from the form and never look "tacked on." Join the bottom of the handle to the lower scored surface in the same manner. Smooth with a damp sponge where needed.

To attach the handle, score the mug and handle at points of attachment. Apply slip to the scorings. Press the top of the handle to the upper scored surface, anchoring it firmly to the pot. Join the bottom of the handle to the lower scored surface. Blend the handle into the form. *(Photograph by Howard M. Berliant)*

Step 5: Cover the piece with a sheet of plastic or plastic bag to permit slow drying. If the pot dries too quickly, cracks may form where the handle is attached to the pot. Dry. Fire and glaze.

Variations

Variation 1: The pulled handle may be attached directly to the leather-hard pot without allowing the handle to dry first. Here, the handle is formed and then attached immediately to the scored top of the form. The handle is bent to shape right on the pot itself. The bottom point of attachment is also scored and the bottom of the handle is attached. While this procedure sometimes achieves greater fluidity of line, it is often tricky to manipulate a wet handle without distorting its form.

Variation 2: For smaller pieces such as mugs, a handle may be pulled directly on the pot. Here the tapered coil of wedged clay is attached firmly to the deeply scored top of the piece. (If the handle piece is not joined securely, it may come off as you are pulling the handle.) The handle is then pulled. as described initially, right on the pot. Excess length is pinched off the bottom of the handle, which is attached to the scored area at the bottom of the piece.

A handle may be pulled directly on the pot. (*Photograph by Howard M. Berliant*)

Try all these methods. You may prefer one particular technique for most of your handles or you may use various methods for different types of pieces.

MAKING A PITCHER

Step 1: Throw a large modified cylinder or bottle shape. (See pages 136–140 and 144–146.)

Step 2: Form a pouring lip on the wet piece. To do this, place the fingers of one hand on the inside of the rim at the place where you want the pitcher to pour. With the thumb and forefinger of the other hand, stroke this area with a pulling motion, enclosing the inside fingers between the two outside fingers to form the pouring spout. Give the spout a slight downstroke to facilitate pouring. Blend the spout into the outside of the form to make a unified whole, stroking its lines into the body of the pot.

Step 3: Allow the form to dry until it is leatherhard. Trim. Shape a handle and allow it to dry slightly. Then attach according to the procedures outlined above. Or attach the wet handle directly to the pot without letting it dry first. Generally it is best not to pull a handle on the pot itself in a larger form. A large handle will keep its shape better if it is allowed to firm up slightly before being fitted to the basic form.

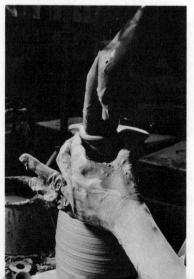

To form a pouring lip on a pitcher, place the fingers of one hand on the inside of the rim at the place where you want the pitcher to pour. With the thumb and forefinger of the other hand, stroke this area with a pulling motion, enclosing the inside fingers between the outside fingers to form the spout. *(Photograph by Howard M. Berliant)*

THROWING A LID

A casserole or other lidded piece is usually made by throwing a bowl form, carefully measuring its inside circumference, and throwing a second bowl to fit inside the first. A knob or other handle is affixed to the top section to facilitate lifting it on and off the pot.

To make a lidded form, you will need calipers to measure the width of the pieces. Calipers may be purchased at a ceramic supply shop.

Always throw a piece and its lid at the same time and use the same type of clay for both parts. If the pieces are thrown at different times or the moisture content of the clay varies significantly, the lid will often not fit the bottom. The lid described here fits inside the rim of the pot. It is called an inset lid. Other types of lids can be thrown to fit over a high rim. Flanged lids may be made to rest inside an opening that does not have a rim or where an especially stable fit is required, as in a teapot. The shape of the lid should be adapted to conform to the piece into or over which it must fit.

MAKING A CASSEROLE
(Inset Lid)

Step 1: Throw a bowl according to the procedure for making this form. Use your thumb to make a strong lip for supporting the lid.

Step 2: Measure the inside width of the bowl with calipers. Measure very carefully, since the lid must conform exactly. If your measurement is off even a little, the lid may be too large and not fit the bottom piece, or too small and fall in.

Step 3: Now throw another bowl. Its outside width must match the measurements of the inside rim of the first bowl. Measure with calipers to see that it conforms exactly. If it does not fit, adjust the

(Above, left) Measure the inside width of the bowl with calipers. (Photograph by Howard M. Berliant)

(Above, right) Throw another bowl that will be the casserole's lid. Its outside width must match the measurements of the inside rim of the first bowl. (Photograph by Howard M. Berliant)

shape, pulling the rim out a bit or pushing it in, again measuring with your calipers to ensure proper dimensions.

Step 4: Allow both pieces to dry to the leather-hard stage. Trim the bottom of the first bowl, adding a foot if you desire. Trim the second bowl, keeping in mind that this will be turned upside down to form the cover of the lidded piece. Remember also that the piece will work as a unit, so top and bottom must harmonize.

Step 5: When the second piece is inverted on the first piece, the two should fit together properly if the measurements were taken carefully. The bottom and the lid should be allowed to dry with the lid placed on the bottom piece, as it will be when the casserole is in use. They should also be fired in this manner. Drying and firing a lidded piece as a unit will reduce warping and ensure proper fit. When glazing a form with a lid, do not put glaze on the area where the lid and bottom touch. Otherwise the glaze will fuse the two sections.

KNOBS

A casserole or other lidded piece needs a handle so that the cover may be easily lifted. A thrown knob makes an excellent handle for a thrown pot. A pulled handle, often shaped into a loop, provides another suitable way of gripping the pot. Of course, other techniques may be used to make handles, as long as they fit the basic design of the pot.

Step 1: To form a thrown knob to use as a lifting device for a thrown cover, center the inverted, leather-hard, trimmed piece, which will be the lid, on the wheel.

Step 2: Score the middle of the lid and firmly attach a small ball of wedged clay at the scored center.

Step 3: Form your knob as you would a small pot, giving it a shape in keeping with the rest of the piece. Make it large enough and high enough for you to grip properly and strong enough to hold the weight of the lid easily.

You may also throw a knob separately, allow it to dry until it is firm enough to handle, and attach

(Above) Score the middle of the lid and firmly attach a small ball of wedged clay at the center. Form it as if you were making a small pot. *(Photograph by Howard M. Berliant)*

(Right) Give the knob a shape in keeping with the rest of the piece. Make it large enough to grip properly. *(Photograph by Howard M. Berliant)*

Finished casserole. The lid fits the bottom bowl. The knob is a proper handle. The total form harmonizes. (Photograph by Howard M. Berliant)

it to the leather-hard finished lid, scoring and using slip. Attach a clay coil at the juncture for added support, blending the knob securely into the lid.

SPOUTS

A wheel-thrown spout is made much in the same way as a small bottle. Thrown spouts are attached primarily to perform a pouring function in creating pieces such as coffeepots and teapots. They can also turn a basic closed-round form into a multi-spouted vase or be used as purely decorative embellishments on other pieces. Spouts should be thrown at the same time as the main piece from the same type of clay with the same moisture content.

Step 1: Make a small bottle in the shape you wish your spout to have. Make the form somewhat taller than the length of the spout, allowing for cutting and fitting the spout to the pot.

Make a small bottle in the shape you wish your spout to have. (Photograph by Howard M. Berliant)

Shape and trim the spout to fit the pot.
(Photograph by Howard M. Berliant)

Step 2: Allow the spout to dry until it can be handled easily. With a cutting wire or sharp knife, sever it from the bat, at an angle if it will be used against the rounded sides of a pot (in making a teapot or coffeepot) or straight across if it will be placed on a flat surface. Cut a hole of proper size in the main form in the area where the spout will be attached (for a coffeepot, vinegar cruet, or multi-spouted vase). Trim or carve spout if desired.

A clay coil may be added at the juncture for added *strength.* (Photograph by Howard M. Berliant)

Step 3: Attach the spout to the main leather-hard, trimmed form, scoring and using slip. A clay coil may be added at the juncture to provide further stability. Smooth the joints with a modeling tool and your fingers.

Step 4: Cover the form with plastic and allow it to dry thoroughly. Fire and glaze.

Pierce holes in the area where the spout will be attached. (Photograph by Howard M. Berliant)

When making a teapot or other complex form, several pieces are thrown separately and joined together. Each piece must fit the other in shape, size, and design. Careful measuring is necessary so that lids will be the correct size. Spouts and handles must perform their function as well as add to, rather than detract from, the design of the piece. When making complex forms like these, it is a good idea, especially initially, to make some sketches of the entire finished piece and to follow these sketches when throwing the separate components.

If you are making a teapot, it will be necessary to pierce holes in the area where the spout will be attached to allow the liquid to pour freely and also to strain out the tea leaves. Be sure to make the holes large enough in size for the pot to pour efficiently.

Finished teapot. Made by Judy Bursak. (Photograph by Howard M. Berliant)

Handles, knobs, lids, and spouts widen the possibilities of creating pottery to fulfill many functions. As your work on the wheel becomes more proficient, you will develop new ideas for adapting the basic symmetrical round form. Paddling with a board before the pot is quite leather-hard can give a round form a flattened or otherwise changed appearance. Pinching a wet piece provides another variation. Squeezing certain areas of the pot with your fingers to form a particular shape is a third alternative. Adding hand-built pieces to the thrown form changes its character again. Throwing several smaller pots and joining them together at the leather-hard stage is a way of making large constructions that the beginner on the wheel would find difficult to handle in one step. Many smaller clay pots can also be made, cut, distorted, and joined to make a free-form thrown sculpture. The potter's wheel, as other clay techniques, provides infinite variations upon a basic theme. Here are three simple experiments to get you started on your departure from the conventional, simple, round wheel form.

14

VARYING THE BASIC WHEEL FORM

WHEEL-THROWN OWL

Wheel-thrown abstract owl. By the author. *(Photograph by Howard M. Berliant)*

Step 1: Form a clay ball into a cylinder that is pushed out slightly in the middle.

Step 2: Cut away any unevenness from the rim with a needle.

Step 3: Pinch the wet form together on top, closing the cylinder.

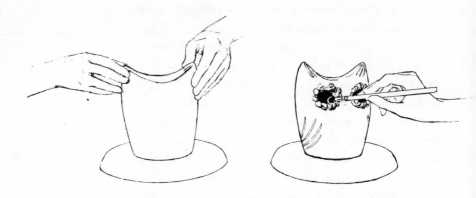

Step 4: With a sharp tool, poke eyes into the owl, pulling out the clay to form lashes. Make the eyes large.

Step 5: Model a small beak and attach. (No scoring is needed with very wet clay.)

Step 6: With a pencil or other sharp pointed tool scratch feathers, wing marks, and other features into the owl.

Step 7: Trim all excess clay from the bottom of the bat. The owl should need no further trimming after it is removed from the wheel.

Step 8: Allow the form to dry. Fire and glaze.

Note: Owls may be made in the manner described above for use as decorative pieces. The cylinder may be thrown without a bottom to make an owl that fits over a candle (the candle shines through the owl's eyes) or for use as an incense burner. A hole may be added at the top of an owl (made with bottom) and the piece hung as a patio decoration, or a clapper may be added (owl without bottom) to make an owl bell.

Wheel-thrown piggy bank.
By the author. *(Photograph
by Howard M. Berliant)*

THROWN PIGGY BANK

Step 1: Throw a fat bottle with a short neck.

Step 2: Trim all excess clay from the base of the bat, giving the bottle its final form.

Step 3: Pinch the rim of the bottle together slightly into a modified figure-eight shape. This will be the pig's snout.

Step 4: Allow the bottle to dry until it is firm enough to handle easily.

Step 5: Model ears, legs, and a tail from small pieces of clay. Attach them to the pig at the proper places, scoring the clay if necessary. Blend modeled parts into main form carefully. Flatten the bottoms of the feet if necessary to be sure the pig stands securely.

Step 6: Cut a slit somewhat longer and wider than

a fifty-cent piece at the top of the pig. Allow for shrinkage.

Step 7: Cover the form with plastic and allow to dry slowly.

Note: This bank is an excellent gift for a child. Money can be poured out of the snout for repeated counting without breaking the pig.

SECTIONAL CONSTRUCTIONS

If you wish to make a form larger than your talents at this time allow, try building it out of several thrown pots joined together. The sectioning can be made obvious, or the parts can be so well blended that no one but you will know the truth. A sectional form is also an excellent project for combining dif-

Sectional construction. Totem pole with modeled features, thrown in three sections. By the author. (*Photograph by Howard M. Berliant*)

rent techniques in one piece, letting each contribute its characteristic texture or form. For example, you might throw the bottom section of the piece, coil the middle section, and again throw the top section. Here, the smooth fluid appearance of the thrown parts would form an interesting counterpoint to the heavily textured broken design of the coils.

In making a sectional creation, (1) be sure to throw (or otherwise construct) all pieces at the same time from the same type of clay with similar moisture content; (2) measure each piece carefully with calipers where the pots are to be joined; be sure each fits the other exactly; (3) when the pieces are leatherhard, trim if necessary; attach one piece to another, scoring and using slip; and (4) blend sections into each other to form a unified whole.

When joining several parts, it is advisable to make a sketch of how you want the finished piece to look, and to think of the total form.

When throwing a pot where each section must sit directly on the one below it, try to keep constant the wall thicknesses of all the pieces. It is generally inadvisable to try to join two pieces where the wall of one is significantly different in thickness from the wall of the other.

Now that you have studied many techniques of creating clay pieces, you may want to combine other hand-building methods with wheel work. Slab pieces especially are often greatly enhanced by the addition of thrown parts—thrown pieces enhanced by adding hand-built parts.

15

DECORATING TECHNIQUES— PRE-FIRING

The treatment of the pot between its initial shaping and its final firing often spells the difference between success and failure. Just as there are many ways of shaping a ceramic piece, there are a variety of techniques used in decorating it. Some methods are best used while the clay is still moist, others when the form has become leather-hard, and still others after the pot has been bisque-fired.

For most pottery, the final (and in some cases only) decorative process will be the use of glaze, applied both to seal the pot and add a final coating of color. A ceramic piece generally assumes its total character only after it has been glazed and then fired for the second time. Of course, there are some instances, as in making flower pots and other pieces, where porosity is desired, when the glaze firing is omitted.

Glazing and decorating are two intimately related and overlapping processes. While the glaze may provide color, texture, and design to the finished piece, any decoration applied to the pot before glazing will affect, often radically, the appearance of the glaze that covers it. For purposes of simplicity, this book will describe decorative processes in two basic categories—those that precede the actual glaze application and those that involve glazing itself. The former will be dealt with in this chapter, the latter in the next chapter.

In making a piece of pottery, you must keep in mind at all times that you are creating a form involving three basic aspects of a process: shaping, designing, and coloring. The shape of the piece, the decorative processes utilized upon it, and the color and texture that it is finally given must all function in harmony, each contributing its own value to the total finished form. A very simple bowl becomes a lovely artistic creation with the addition of interesting decoration and suitable glaze, while another beautifully crafted piece may completely lose its positive qualities by poorly applied decorative processes.

Decoration and glazing are the steps beginners tend to neglect most frequently. Once the pot is thrown or otherwise finished in form, it is, to them, complete. "Slap some glaze on and be done with it" is the attitude taken by many novices. Instructors try to counteract this attitude, generally to little avail. It is often not until the beginner himself transcends the point of wanting to create quantity that he shifts his emphasis toward the quality of the total, finished product. In order to avoid a collection of haplessly glazed and decorated pottery, familiarize yourself with the following techniques and then spend some time in learning them well. Here again, as in other aspects of clay work, executing and practicing each method conscientiously will pay rewarding dividends in rapid progress, and beautifully finished pieces.

To test out the various decorative processes that follow, it is advisable to make some tiles and experiment on these with different forms of decoration. After they have been fired, you will have a concrete idea of what to expect from each process and can apply these techniques with some practical knowledge in the decoration of finished pots. As you become more expert in this area of pottery, you will develop your own preferred techniques and may not use some of those listed here at all. Still, at the beginning, it is advisable to try each one at least once to acquaint yourself with as many different avenues of decoration as possible.

PROCESSES USED ON WET CLAY

Many of the processes used on wet clay have been described in previous chapters. After a thrown pot has been formed on the wheel, it can be pinched or pressed to change its shape. When it is almost leather-hard, it may be paddled to modify, alter, or distort its form. It may also be textured or decorated by the methods described below.

In Chapter 5, you experimented with a wide variety of textures that could be created using your fingers or available household articles. These can, of course, be applied with equal success to various finished forms of pottery.

Impressed Decorations

Here the clay is imprinted with a tool or other object that can be pressed into the moist surface to make a design—paper clips, string, hair curlers, plaster or clay stamps, fragments of fossils or seashells, letters from a child's printing set, and bark, to name only a few. The clay may also be scratched with a tool, fork tines, fingernails, or textured by using pressure from your fingers, knuckles, and hands. This type of texturing should be done while the clay is still damp. If the piece becomes too hard, it will not be very malleable and the designs will not "take" as well. Pressing an object into a hardened surface may cause the clay to crack.

Mug with impressed decoration. Japanese printing block was used achieve this design. Made by Mich Cole. (Photograph by Howard M. B liant)

Thrown and slab-built pot with carved texture. This design was made by incising. Made by Michele Cole. *(Photograph by Howard M. Berliant)*

und form with added clay dec-
ation. Reduction fired. Made by
n Hotek. Antonio Prieto Collec-
n of Modern Ceramics, Mills Col-
ge. *(Photograph by Margaret
Hamer)*

Adding Clay

While the form is still moist, additional clay may be applied to form a raised design that adds to the textural qualities of the piece. Plastic clay may be laid on in decorative patterns. Moist clay may be pressed through a sieve and the "strings" cut with a sharp knife to provide "hair" or other string-like textures. While many of these techniques may also be used on leather-hard clay, they require no scoring and need only be pressed on firmly when used on a moist surface.

PROCESSES USED ON
LEATHER-HARD CLAY

Carving

Clay may be carved in its leather-hard state either by incising or excising a design into its surface. These methods are best used at this stage since the clay cuts cleanly and will not stick to the carving tool. When clay is incised, a pattern is cut into the clay. This leaves the surrounding clay its original thickness, while the incised area (pattern) is lowered.

When the clay is excised a pattern is carved out

of the clay. This raises the pattern and lowers the area surrounding it.

To carve clay, use a sharp tool—a knife or wire-loop tool for larger excised areas, a pointed cutting tool or sharpened pencil for incised patterns. Dental tools are excellent for carving clay, and you might prevail upon your dentist to save you some of his cast-off tools.

Appliqués

Designs may be cut from plastic clay, allowed to dry until they can be handled without distortion, and then applied to the leather-hard form; score and use slip. This is a simple way to add a significantly raised design to your piece. Blend the appliqué into the main piece with a modeling tool so that it adheres to the piece firmly. Smooth with your fingers and a damp sponge if necessary. For subtle raising, designs may be excised. For more obvious depth contrast, appliqués are added. After applying a modeled or appliquéd design, cover the piece with plastic and allow it to dry slowly. Otherwise the design may separate from the main piece.

Pots with appliqué designs. Made by the author (left) and Peggy King (right). *(Photograph by Howard M. Berliant)*

Slip Decoration

Colored slips are clays in liquid form to which coloring oxides have been added. They are applied under glazes and used in various decorating methods. They are generally put on unfired pottery, often when the clay is leather-hard. Another name for these colored slips is engobe. While these two terms are generally interchangeable, some engobes contain glaze-forming ingredients to reduce the shrinkage of the clay and provide better adherence to the fired clay form. When using engobes on bisque ware, it is recommended that these vitreous engobes be used.

Coating

An entire piece (inside and/or outside) may be covered with a colored slip, and various techniques may be used to contrast the color of the slip with the natural color of the clay or with the color of the glaze that will be applied before the second firing. Even though engobe is applied before the piece has been fired, it retains its coloring properties through the second firing.

Painting

Engobes may also be used to "paint" a design on leather-hard clay. Here only part of the pot is covered or several different colors are used to cover the entire pot. While a design may also be painted on bisque ware with glazes, these often tend to run. When slip is used, the design stays put. Since slip is thicker and more difficult to work with than ordinary paint, try to keep your design fairly simple. To apply a design with slip, use a "loaded" brush. The porous unfired clay absorbs water at a rapid rate, so be sure to use enough slip to provide an even layer. "Lay" rather than brush the design on

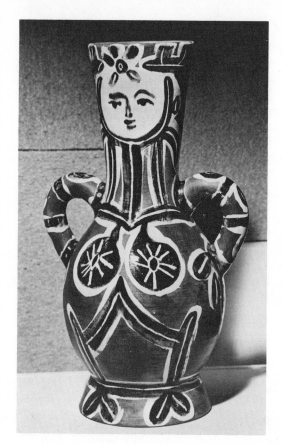

Cast vase in the shape of a woman. Painted with engobes and oxides. Pablo Picasso. Antonio Prieto Collection of Modern Ceramics, Mills College. (Photograph by Howard M. Berliant)

the piece, as drying slip has a tendency to flake. Keep in mind that the engobes will be strongly affected by the glaze applied over them. A transparent or translucent glaze, either clear or colored, will allow the design to show through. This is the type of glaze recommended for use with this technique. An opaque glaze will generally mask the slip. A clear transparent glaze will retain the true colors of engobe and clay. A colored translucent glaze may change the colors (for example, a blue engobe may turn green when used under a yellow glaze).

Engobes may be purchased ready to use at a ceramic supply house, or you may buy coloring oxides separately and add them to slip to obtain the color of your choice. "Raw" engobes are not the same color as they will be after they are fired. If the gray slip in the jar is labeled turquoise, believe the label, not your eyes. Engobes and slips are basically clay, not glass. They provide color but do not substitute for glaze in sealing a pot. The pot is as porous after the use of slips as before their application.

Slip Trailing

As stated previously, slips may be brushed on to coat an entire pot with color or to decorate parts of a surface. They may also be applied in a design

Large vase with slip trailing used as decoration. Eugene Bunker. Antonio Prieto Collection of Modern Ceramics, Mills College. (Photograph by Howard M. Berliant)

by another technique known as "slip trailing" or "tracing." This method utilizes a rubber ear syringe, which may be purchased at any drug store. The syringe is filled with slip, which is then squeezed onto the pot in a pattern.

The design is achieved by movements of the hand controlling the syringe. The slip decoration will be slightly raised from the pot's surface. Slip trailing is especially suited for various types of line decorations.

A plastic ketchup or mustard container with a squirt top or any flexible, easy-to-grasp bottle with a small top opening may be used as a slip trailer. A fabric pastry bag with a thin tip also works well. Slip trailing is most effective on flat surfaces such as platters and low bowls where the design won't run as it is applied. It may also be used on straight-sided pieces, with slightly different results. Many colors of slip can provide interesting variations and contrasts in color and design.

Flat bowl with oxidation and sgraffito decoration. Edwin Scheier. Antonio Prieto Collection of Modern Ceramics, Mills College. *(Photograph by Margaret d'Hamer)*

Sgraffito

Coat the leather-hard pot with a layer of slip. After the slip has dried completely, use a sharp tool to scratch or carve a design into the clay. This will remove part of the slip, exposing the color of the raw clay underneath. The contrast between clay color and slip color within the design provides the interest in this technique. Apply transparent or translucent glaze after bisque firing.

Sgraffito is an Italian word meaning "scratch through." In this technique, the slip must be "scratched" at the proper time. If it becomes too dry, the coating may flake off when the design is incised. If it is not allowed to dry long enough, the design will be "muddy" rather than precise.

DECORATING ON DRY CLAY

While there are some potters who do much of their decorating on dry, unfired clay, this author takes the view that most pieces can be more easily and effectively decorated before firing while the piece is either moist or leather-hard or after the initial bisque-fire. Clay in its dry state is in many ways at its most fragile stage. It has neither the flexibility of moist clay nor the durability of fired ware. It is easily chipped, cracked, and broken in handling. When moisture is applied to it, the ware is likely to crack.

However, if you must decorate your pieces at this stage, they may still be carefully carved, by the methods described on page 172 ("Carving"), and, sponged lightly and decorated with engobes or oxides, or wax resist may be applied as explained in the following chapter.

Slab-built, lidded, hinged mug, made from textured clay. Modeled and macramé decoration. Here another craft form (macramé) is employed to enhance a ceramic piece. Mug by Anni Grundler. (Photograph by Howard M. Berliant)

Pottery may be combined with any number of other crafts media to obtain unusual effects. Macramé may be used to add decoration, as in the mug pictured here, or it may enhance the function of a piece, as when a clay pot is suspended in a macramé hanger to form a hanging planter. Leather is also often used in conjunction with pottery (see clay beads strung on leather to make a necklace, or hanging planter or bells suspended from leather thongs). Leather, too, may add function or decoration. Wood, metal, and different woven materials are also often successfully combined with ceramic pieces. Often several craft media may be used in conjunction, each adding its particular appeal to enhance the other.

Glaze is the clothing of pottery. It is the last step in the act of creation—the potter's final touch that gives the form its finished texture, color, and decoration.

16

GLAZING

THE FUNCTION OF GLAZE

Glaze has two functions. It adds to the decorative qualities of the piece and changes the porous bisque ware into a sealed watertight entity. Glaze is a type of glass. Under the high temperatures of the "glost" or second firing, the glaze melts and fuses with the clay body, coating it with a glasslike covering.

GLAZE COMPOSITION

Glaze is composed of three basic elements—silica, alumina, and flux. Each performs its own functions. Silica (or flint) is the essential glaze ingredient. It is the glass-former. Silica has such a high melting point that even the upper temperatures of the kiln are not sufficient to melt it in its unadulterated form. Therefore, another material, flux, is added to lower the melting point of silica. It makes the glaze ingredients melt and fuse together. The most common types of fluxes used in low-fire glazes are lead oxides and alkaline compounds. The last essential ingredient in glazes is alumina. This adds strength, hardness, and body to the glaze and allows it to be fired to a higher maturing temperature, making it more resistant to shock and abrasion. It helps the glaze adhere to the form. Metallic oxides, such as cobalt, copper, chromium, and manganese, give glazes their color.

These few sentences serve only to give you a very basic and general idea of what makes up a glaze and why each component is necessary. The field of glaze composition and calculation is a complex, technical, and fascinating area. However, it is one that is best explored in detail only after one learns more about the nature of glazes, how to apply them, what happens when they are fired, and what are some of the commonly used glaze techniques.

COMMERCIAL GLAZES

There are many excellent glazes available commercially. While you will undoubtedly want to experiment with creating your own after you become more proficient and adventurous in this area, initially it is far more predictable, simpler, and less frustrating to purchase glazes that are ready to use. Even if you buy prepared products, there are enough variables involved in the interaction of glaze, clay, and firing temperature to make this a constantly fascinating and often unpredictable field.

Whole books have been written on glaze calculation alone. Once you have advanced to the point where you want to create your own glazes, read some of these and follow the specific instructions provided therein. The author strongly recommends that glazes used for all projects at the beginning stages of ceramics be purchased in prepared form from a ceramic supply dealer. Most shops where glazes are sold display a variety of sample tiles that show how the glaze will perform when used on a particular clay at a particular temperature. Consult these samples and pick a glaze that approximates the results you wish to achieve. Always keep in mind that the finished effect will depend on a number of factors. Use the samples only as guides. Don't expect your piece to be an exact color replica of the test tile on which you based your choice.

Glazes come in a variety of colors, transparencies,

and textures. For example—blue (color), opaque (transparency), matte (texture). The color of the glaze is affected by (1) the color of the clay body, (2) the colors of engobes or oxides used with it, (3) the firing temperature of the kiln, and (4) the type of firing—whether the pottery is oxidation- or reduction-fired. The same glaze will react differently on white clay than on red. A light-colored engobe applied under it will modify the glaze in one way, while the application of a dark slip will change its color tones another way. The same glaze fired at a low temperature may look different than when fired at a high temperature. Low-fire glazes will often "fire out" (lose their color) when fired above their maturing temperatures. For example, a red glaze will turn brown if fired above cone 06 (about 1850° F.). High-fire glazes will not reach their full luster when underfired. Reduction firing will change the color of glazes and clay (see the next chapter).

HOW TO CHOOSE GLAZES

Glazes are generally classified according to the three basic properties described previously—color, type (whether the glaze is glossy or matte, opaque, translucent, or transparent), and maturing temperature. When you buy a glaze, there are several important considerations to keep in mind.

1. Choose a glaze that fits your clay body (that is, one that matures at the same temperature as the clay). Do not choose a high-fire glaze for a low-fire clay body—or vice versa. If the clay and glaze are incompatible, defects such as "crazing," cracking, or "shivering" may occur. Glaze that is unsuited to the clay will not fuse properly onto the form. When in doubt, ask. The dealer who sells you the clay and glaze will be able to guide you to compatible selections.

2. Choose a glaze within the firing range of your kiln. If your ware will be fired at low temperatures, it would be unwise to select high-fire stoneware glazes. If the clay will be fired at high temperatures, low-fire glazes will generally give unsatisfactory results. Most glazes have some flexibility in firing range. Be sure to select one that matures at the temperature at which your kiln will be fired.

3. Choose a glaze in color and type that will best enhance your pot. A bright-colored glossy glaze may be extremely attractive on a small smooth vase but may look garish on a large textured pot. Conversely a matte glaze in earth colors might do much to enhance a substantial casserole but may look dull and heavy on a small pot. The glaze should always be in character with the rest of the pot.

4. Choose a glaze suitable for the function of the piece. There has been some discussion about the safety of hand-made pottery ware for use in eating or serving food. Many glazes are safe to use on pots that will hold food. The culprits are glazes containing lead.

Many selling potters display their wares with signs stating "lead-free glazes used." The "lead scare," while perhaps misunderstood by some nonpotters, has a very real basis in fact. Although lead glazes may be safe for use on pottery that does not come into contact with food, such as vases, sculpture, and other decorative pieces, they must not be applied to pieces that hold edibles or touch the mouth. Use only "lead-free" (or "lead-safe") glazes on mugs, dishes, casseroles, and serving bowls. Many manufacturers have a line of leadless glazes prepared especially for food containers.

As mentioned previously, lead oxides are one of the two most commonly used fluxes in low-fire glazes. Lead is extremely poisonous. It requires careful handling even if used on ware that will not come in contact with food. The dust particles themselves can be poisonous when inhaled. The danger of using lead in glazing eating ware is that lead compounds contained in the fired glaze may be dissolved by food chemicals and these poisonous materials may then be ingested.

When you are buying low-fire glazes, substitute alkaline glazes for lead whenever possible. Buy only those labeled "lead-free" or their equivalent for use on food or beverage containers. If you have any doubts, ask. This is not an area in which to take chances.

Glazes may be purchased in powdered form or premixed and ready to use. If you buy powdered glazes, they must first be mixed with water to the "thick cream" consistency. Premixed glazes should be stirred and shaken to ensure even consistency but are otherwise ready to use. Both have their slight advantages, but neither is really preferable. The premixed variety does have the advantage of being completely ready to use as needed.

TEST TILES

After you have selected small amounts of several glazes that fit the clay body and kiln you will be using, make some test tiles. To do this, cut a number of small tiles and fire them. Paint strips of various glazes on each tile. Apply three coats of glaze for each strip. Label each glaze sample with a ceramic crayon or put the glaze number or name on the back of the tile with dark engobe or slip. Have these tiles fired in the kiln in which your other pieces will be fired at the temperatures that will be generally used. Now you have a concrete reference on which to base future glazing. If you know the temperature at which the kiln was fired (or if it is generally heated to the same temperature each time) and use the same glaze and clay body again, your glazes should provide similar results upon successive firings.

When using these and other glazes on your pottery, keep a journal to remind yourself which glazes you used on which pot. Draw a picture of the form in your journal and add all information about glazes, engobes, oxides, methods of decoration, and firing. A record of this kind is immensely valuable to all potters, from beginners to advanced students.

STEPS PRECEDING GLAZING

Pottery is generally glazed by one of four methods: brushing, pouring, dipping, or spraying. Each has its advantages and disadvantages. Some are more suitable for certain forms than others. Whatever method you decide to use, there are some steps that should precede glazing:

Step 1: Any piece that is to be glazed should first be bisque-fired. While it is possible to glaze greenware and fire it to completion in one process, this is a tricky procedure, occasionally done in commercial potteries, which is not suitable for the beginner or the home potter.

Step 2: Wipe the bisque pot thoroughly with a clean damp sponge or rinse it swiftly under running water. This serves a double function. It removes dust and loose particles of clay and causes the piece to absorb some water, making it less porous. Sponged bisque ware will have less tendency to soak up too much glaze. Always wash your hands with soap before handling bisque ware as greasy finger marks left on pots may cause glaze defects in the second firing.

Step 3: Dip the bottom of the pot in melted wax or commercially prepared "wax resist." This will save laborious cleaning of the foot after the pot has been glazed. The wax serves to repel the glaze and keep the foot glaze-free. Glaze left on the bottom of the form may run off the pot onto the kiln and fuse the two together, ruining both the piece and the kiln shelf in the process.

Step 4: Mix powdered glaze to heavy-cream consistency or stir premixed glaze to uniform thickness.

METHODS OF GLAZING

After the pot has been prepared by the preceding steps, glaze, using one of the following methods. It is generally best to glaze the inside of the pot first, especially if you will use dipping or pouring as the method of application.

Brushing

Brushing is probably the most widely used technique for beginners working at home. It requires less glaze than dipping or pouring and less equipment than spraying to provide satisfactory results. It may be used on any pieces except on the inside of those with thin long necks, in which case, pouring is the only really workable technique. Brushing is especially suitable for large pieces, which may be difficult to pour or dip. Use a large flat brush, about 1-inch wide to apply the glaze.

Two to three coats of glaze are applied to the pot with short, even strokes of the brush. When glazing the outside of a piece, apply the first coat of glaze almost to the bottom (say ¼ inch from the bottom). The second coat should end about ¼ inch above the first coat; the third coat about ¼ inch above the second. Glaze has a tendency to run. If the glaze is applied too heavily at the bottom of a pot, it may run right off into the kiln, causing disaster for both pot and kiln shelf. That is why each successive coat is best ended a bit above the

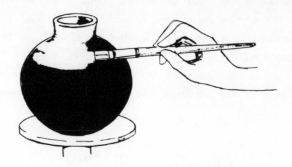

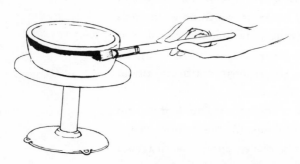

one preceding it. Wait for each coat to dry slightly before applying the next. This is necessary for the glaze to adhere properly. Do not wait until the glaze is too dry, and do not let your pot stand more than a few minutes before applying a second or third coat. If one layer is too dry before the other is applied, this may cause defects in the glaze firing.

Try to brush the glaze on as evenly as possible. It is almost impossible to achieve complete uniformity of glaze application by brushing. Since the glaze has a tendency to run, this works to your advantage, as it will mask its own slight unevenness of application. Glaze should be applied a bit more heavily at the top of the piece and less heavily at the bottom for reasons that should be self-evident by now. If some glaze does run onto the waxed foot it may be easily sponged off. In any method of glazing, always be sure to check that all glaze is removed from the foot of the pot before it is placed in the kiln.

Pouring

Glazes used for pouring or dipping should be somewhat thinner in consistency than those used in brushing, since these two techniques leave a thicker layer on the pot. Pouring is the best technique to use to ensure an even coating on the inside of a pot. Its one drawback is that it uses somewhat more glaze than brushing. Its advantages are that it provides an even-layered glaze and is a much quicker method to use than brushing. Pouring requires only a one-step operation. Brushing requires two or three coats. Pouring is also particularly suitable for certain types of forms. For instance, the inside of a tall narrow bottle would be extremely difficult to glaze in any other manner.

To pour a glaze, fill the inside of the form about one-half to three-quarters full. Quickly swish the glaze around inside the piece, covering most of the inside. Tilt the pot, and pour out the glaze, revolving the form so that glaze completely coats all parts of the inside. Pour the glaze into a container you have provided for this purpose. Some speed is required here or the glaze will form too

thick a buildup on the walls of the pot and may cause cracks or other defects when the pot is fired.

While pouring is most often used on the inside of a container, glaze may be poured over the outside of a form as well. The best way to do this is to place the pot on two wooden strips (after having glazed the inside) over a large container, which catches the excess poured glaze. Invert the form on wooden supports and pour glaze over the outside, covering all areas uniformly. Excess glaze will run off the sides into the container beneath the form. Clean off any glaze that adheres to the foot with a clean wet sponge.

To pour glaze on a bottle or other form that is difficult to invert in the above manner, hold the bottle by the neck or foot and pour glaze as indi-

cated above. Touch up any finger marks (where bottle was grasped) with a brush.

Pouring and brushing may be used on the same pot. It is often easiest and most desirable to pour the inside of a form, allow it to dry, and then brush the glaze onto the outside.

Dipping

Dipping requires more glaze than either brushing or pouring. For this procedure, fill a container with an amount of glaze sufficient in depth to cover at least half the pot. If enough glaze is available for total submersion, hold by the foot and dip it into the glaze for a few seconds to coat it completely. Shake to remove excess glaze. If the piece does not have a graspable foot, it may be held with tongs while it is immersed. Touch up the tong marks by brushing them when the pot is removed from the glaze.

If you do not have sufficient glaze to immerse the entire piece, you may dip one half, remove the piece and allow the glaze to dry slightly, and then

dip the unglazed half. If the glaze overlaps slightly in the middle, this provides a subtle attractive color depth variation. Wipe any excess glaze off the waxed foot with a clean damp sponge. While dipping requires more glaze than the techniques previously mentioned, it is a simple, effective one-step method of glazing pottery.

Spraying

There are special spray guns available for spraying glaze. These may be purchased at a ceramic supply house. If a professional glaze gun is not available, a spraying apparatus that works on the aerosol bomb principle may be used. Even a flit gun will sometimes do a satisfactory job. Glaze used for this method must be thinned sufficiently so that it will come through the small holes without clogging the apparatus.

Spraying produces a thin even coat of glaze and may be used to obtain subtle variations in color. Unlike dipping or pouring, which allow a fairly heavy application in one step, it produces a fragile thin film on the pot. Two or three layers of sprayed glaze are usually necessary to provide an even coat. Even then, the fragile coating provided by this process is easily damaged before the pot is fired—so handle with care. The thickness of the glaze may be checked by scratching through the coating with your fingernail or a sharp tool. The glaze should be about 1/16-inch thick. Heal the scratch by rubbing over it with your finger.

In using this method, be sure to spray only in a well-ventilated area, as the spraying process fills

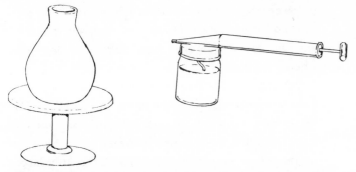

the air with sometimes toxic vapors (as in the case of lead glazes). Even if the vapors are not toxic, inhaling is not recommended. Spraying necessitates equipment not required by other methods. It is generally used where other techniques will not work as well, as in glazing large pieces or for achieving subtle color effects. It may, however, be used on almost any form except the inside of a piece with an inaccessible interior, like a long thin bottle.

GLAZE DECORATION

Any of the above-mentioned methods may be used to provide an even coating of glaze on the finished bisqued pot. If you have used another technique before the first firing, you will probably want to leave your glaze intact. If you have used no other decorative techniques before the pot was bisqued, you may want to design the basic glaze coating further by one of the following methods.

Engobes

While engobes are used primarily on leather-hard clay, they may also be used on bisque ware. When purchasing engobes for use on fired clay, be sure to tell the dealer how you plan to use them, so he will supply you with a vitreous engobe that is partly glaze and partly clay. These engobes have a lower-than-usual proportion of clay so that they will not shrink away from the bisqued pot and enough fluxes to make them adhere to the form when it is fired.

Designs are brushed onto bisque ware much as onto leather-hard clay. Engobes are used mainly to provide variations in glaze color. For example, a pot banded in blue-green, green, and blue engobes will show subtle shading when a translucent turquoise glaze is used over the whole pot. Engobe designs painted on a piece will remain constant. Glaze applied over them will not alter the design. Use engobes under glazes, glaze over engobes.

Sgraffito

The sgraffito technique may be used to scratch designs through glaze on a bisqued pot much in the same way it was used to scratch through slip on a leather-hard piece.

First glaze the pot. With a sharp tool, cut or scratch a design into the glaze. The unglazed clay will be exposed in the scratched areas. If the raw clay was initially coated with colored slips or engobes (totally or in part), sgraffito will reveal the slipped color under the glaze.

Casserole. Sgraffito through glaze. Reduction fired. Made by Antonio Prieto, courtesy Eunice Prieto. *(Photograph by Margaret d'Hamer)*

While the technique used for sgraffito on leather-hard clay and on bisque ware is much the same, the results vary somewhat. When this method is used to scratch through slip, the design made by the tool stays just as it was incised and remains constant even after the bisque-firing. When you use this technique with glaze rather than slip, the carved design will often not be as precise after firing. While slip "stays put" in the kiln, glaze runs. However, the amount of running varies according to the type of glaze. Generally a matte opaque glaze will run only very slightly, while a glossy transparent one may run a great deal. In using sgraffito to scratch through glaze, be sure to use glazes that run minimally.

Wax Resist

This technique uses a thin layer of melted wax as a tool to repel glaze. A design is brushed onto the pot with melted wax. The pot is glazed as usual.

(Above, left) Bowl with wax-resist decoration. By Judy Bursak. (Photograph by Howard M. Berliant)

(Above, right) Face bottle. Peter Voulkas. Oxide, sgraffito, and wax-resist decoration. Antonio Prieto Collection of Modern Ceramics, Mills College. (Photograph by Howard M. Berliant)

The wax repels or "resists" the glaze in the area where it was applied. Thus, glaze adheres to the nonwaxed parts of the pot and pulls away from sections that are coated with wax. Three common uses of this technique follow.

1. Wax resist may be brushed onto a bisqued pot and glaze applied over it, allowing the natural clay (or slip color) to show through. The area where wax was applied remains unglazed.

2. A pot may be partially glazed, wax resist applied over the first glaze, and a second glaze put on the remainder of the pot. Here, the wax protects the first glaze and keeps the second one from covering it.

3. Glaze may be applied to the total piece and the whole pot then covered with a thin layer of wax. Sgraffito may be used in conjunction with the wax. A sharp tool is used to scratch or carve through the wax and glaze, exposing areas of unglazed clay. The pot is now reglazed. The second glaze covers only the clay that was exposed by scratching, since the rest is still protected by the

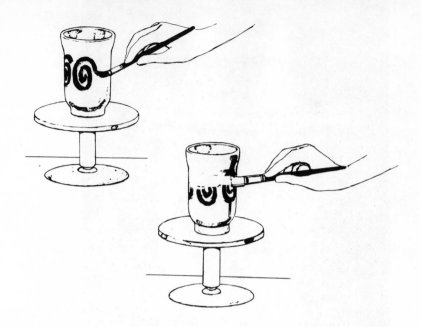

wax. You now have a pot with one glaze used as background and the other to fill in the scratched design.

Any melted wax may be used for the wax resist technique. Melted paraffin or beeswax are quite suitable. Commercially prepared, inexpensive wax resist may be bought at ceramic supply shops. It has the advantage of staying in liquid, ready-to-use form, thus saving the trouble of melting wax for each use.

Oxides or Stains

Colored oxides or stains may be brushed onto a bisqued pot before or after it is glazed. These colorants can be purchased in powdered form at your ceramic supply dealer. You add the powder to a little water, then mix to desired consistency. The less water added, the stronger the color. For extreme color, oxides may be patted lightly onto the moist glazed pot in their dry form. For very subtle color, they may be thinned to water-color consist-

Large thrown and slab bottle. Oxide and sgraffito decoration. Antonio Prieto. (*Photograph by Howard M. Berliant*)

ency and applied with a brush. Oxides may be
applied dry, cream consistency, somewhat thinner
than cream, water-color consistency, and so on,
depending on the intensity of color desired. Too
thick an application will cause the oxides to become
metallic and burn the glaze.

Oxides are used to add color under or over a
glaze. An oxide applied below the glaze will give
more subtle color effects. An oxide applied over the
glaze produces more intense color. Some common
oxides that you may want to try include iron oxide,

which produces colors ranging from beige to reddish brown to dark brown; copper, ranging from turquoise to green; cobalt, various shades of blue; and manganese, purple to brown. Inquire which oxides will provide the color effects you wish to produce.

While oxides are often applied on bisque ware, they may also be used on moist or leather-hard clay. When oxides are used on fired clay, the details remain sharp. If used on unfired clay, they are softened by the moisture content of the clay.

Frit

Frit is ground glass. It may be purchased from a ceramic supply dealer in powdered form. There is one type of frit that may also be used as a deco-

Bowl by Peggy King. Special frit (see text) used for decoration to cause crackle effect and pooling. (Photograph by Howard M. Berliant)

rating technique, to produce pooling of colors and sometimes a crackle effect. This type of frit is generally known as frit 25 but may go by somewhat different numbers depending upon the manufacturer.

For this type of decoration, a thick layer of frit 25 (about ¼-inch in depth) is used in conjunction with several glazes. Glossy, art, or crackle glazes are recommended. The frit causes the glazes to run into each other and pool at the bottom of a bowl or other slightly sloping container, sometimes with a "crackle" effect. This running together of glazes provides a blurred, subtle, almost watercolor-like effect. The frit contributes added gloss to the piece. Frit is best used on the inside of a sloping container in conjunction with several glossy glazes.

Luster Decoration

Luster is a form of decoration in which a thin metallic film appears on the surface of the glazed piece. It is an over-glaze decoration and is applied to a pot that has already been glaze-fired.

Lusters may be purchased in prepared form from a ceramic supply dealer in such colors as gold, silver, and pearl. They are applied over a glazed pot by painting or spraying. The pot is then fired to red heat (about 1600° F. or cone 012) whereby ingredients within the luster react to create the metallic film. While lusters were originally used by Persian potters in a reducing fire, today's commercial preparations (or those you make yourself) contain ingredients that enable them to be fired in a low-fire electric kiln or in a gas kiln using an oxidation firing. So lusters may be used in an oxidation or reduction kiln.

To sum up glaze techniques, a pot may be glazed

Bowl with glaze trailing decoration. Antonio Prieto.
(Photograph by Howard M. Berliant)

Large vase by Antonio Prieto. This form is
partially glazed and partially unglazed. *(Photograph by Howard M. Berliant)*

Cookie jar with overlapping poured glaze decoration. By Peggy King. (Photograph by Howard M. Berliant)

Donut bottle with dripped glaze decoration. By the author. (Photograph by Howard M. Berliant)

simply by brushing, pouring, dipping, or spraying an even coating of glaze on its surface. This glaze may also be varied by one of the techniques just mentioned. Glazes may be used for glaze trailing as slip was used for slip trailing. Several glazes may be used side by side or overlapped to again vary the colors of the pot. When using more than one glaze on the same piece, be sure that each glaze fits the clay body and that all glazes mature at the same temperature. Glazes must interact harmoniously with each other and with the piece to which they are applied.

Whichever method of glazing you use, be sure to check the bottom of each pot before it is fired to make sure no glaze adheres to the foot.

EGYPTIAN PASTE

Egyptian paste is a self-glazing low-fire body particularly suited to making jewelry and other miniature objects. It is included in this chapter because glaze is an essential part of its composition. It is, however, a unique product, requiring no additional glazing since it glazes itself in the firing process. In ancient Egypt, faience (or what we now call Egyptian paste) was used to make some of the earliest glazed ware in the history of ceramics. Jewelry, ornaments, and miniature figures of gods, people, and animals were its most common forms of usage. Jewelry made from faience was greatly valued by the early Egyptians. Some beautiful pieces, mainly in varying shades of turquoise may still be seen in museums around the country.

Today's craftsmen have not been able to duplicate exactly the ancient Egyptian formula for this clay-glass composition but have come up with materials that closely resemble the original. Egyptian paste may be made according to several specific formulas for which a variety of ingredients and a gram scale are required. Most recipes are basically a mixture of clay and soda with copper oxide added as a colorant. When you have advanced into creating glazes of your own and are familiar with glaze calculation, you may make your own Egyptian paste using the methods similar to those by which you create your glazes. At this point, however, it is best to buy ready-made Egyptian paste from your ceramic supply dealer. This is usually purchased in powdered form to which water is added according to the instructions supplied with the material.

Egyptian paste is a material particularly suited for making jewelry since it is light-weight and fires to a variety of beautiful colors. The most popular colors are in the blue-to-green families, resembling the colors of the original Egyptian ware. However, it may also be purchased in yellow, white, terra cotta, black, purple, and dark blue. Since the material is self-glazing, half the work is immediately eliminated. One need only form the pieces and they will glaze themselves in the kiln. Anyone who has spent time glazing small objects like beads and buttons will appreciate the advantages of a one-step process.

Since Egyptian paste is actually a combination of clay and glazes, it is not as plastic as clay and suitable only for small simple forms that do not require extreme malleability.

To make Egyptian paste jewelry:

1. Buy commercially prepared Egyptian paste powder in your choice of colors. Add sufficient water to form a claylike consistency (or use formulas available in several ceramics books). Knead the material until it is pliable. If it crumbles, add a bit more water.

2. Now make the beads, jewelry pieces, or small

Faience Ushabti (small god figure). (Photograph courtesy of the Rosicrucian Egyptian Museum).

Faience necklace. (Photograph courtesy Rosicrucian Egyptian Museum)

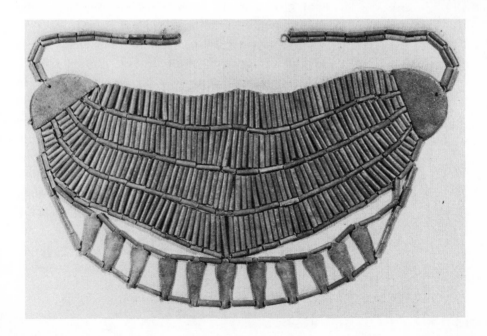

sculptures according to any desired method. Since the plasticity of this material is limited, the simpler the process and the finished piece, the better the results.

In making beads, you may roll a coil and slice off one bead at a time. Or roll round beads in the palm of your hand. For all projects, keep the paste that is not immediately in use covered with plastic so that it does not dry out.

3. When making jewelry, use a long nail to poke holes in your pieces. String beads on a wire as soon as they are firm enough to hold their shape. (If you string them on nichrome wire or dry them on a bead rack, they may be placed right in the kiln without further handling once they are completely dry. Firing beads is discussed in more detail in the following chapter.)

You will notice that a sugary coating develops on the surface of the forms as the paste dries. This will melt in the kiln to become the glaze for the piece. Be careful not to disturb this deposit. If it is brushed off accidentally, there will be no glaze on that area of the piece where it was removed.

4. There are some formulas for Egyptian paste that give a matte finish. Here the beads may be fired together in a bowl without danger of their sticking together. However most commercial pastes and other formulas give a glossy glazelike finish. Thoroughly dry beads must be strung on nichrome wires or bead racks far enough apart so they will not touch to prevent them from fusing together in the kiln. The wires may be coated with kiln wash to prevent the beads from sticking to them. In preparing beads or other pieces for firing, handle them with care and try not to disturb their glaze coating.

5. Commercial pastes fired to cone 06 (low-fire earthenware temperatures) will develop glassy finishes and sometimes crackle effects. Most Egyptian

pastes are fired between cone 010 (1640° F.) and cone 04 (1940° F.).

COMMON GLAZE FLAWS

Glazes do not always live up to the potter's expectations. This is true not only for the novice but also for the craftsman who has spent many years in the field of ceramics. Glaze flaws may be due to a variety of reasons. They may arise from problems in the way the glaze was mixed or applied, problems in firing, or incompatibility of clay and glaze. The same flaw may occur for different reasons (see "crazing," below). It is not always easy to determine which variable caused a particular fault.

Here are a few of the most common defects that occur in glazing. If your pot shows one or more of them, try to pinpoint your difficulties and attempt, as much as possible, to avoid the same pitfalls in your next glaze experience.

1. *Crackling* or *"crazing"* may take place for several different reasons. Crazing usually occurs when the glaze and clay body do not fit each other. The glaze shrinks more than the clay. Tiny cracks on the surface of the pot may also be due to too-heavy glaze application. If the drying glaze cracks on the unfired pot, these cracks will often become more pronounced when the piece is fired. Next time, use less glaze. Crazing may also occur if the pot is cooled too quickly (taken out hot from an insufficiently cooled kiln and exposed to cold air), if several glazes that mature at different temperatures are used, or if the piece is underfired.

2. *"Crawling."* In this defect, the glaze "moves" away from certain areas of the pot, leaving them unglazed, and bunches in thick clumps in other areas. This may be due to dust or oil on the bisqued

surface. To avoid crawling, rinse or sponge your pot and do not handle it more than necessary. Unwashed hands often leave greasy finger marks on bisqued pieces. Crawling is often caused by too-heavy glaze application that cracks upon drying or by firing the pot before the glaze has dried.

3. *Pinholes* or *blisters*. These may occur if the bisque ware was not sponged before glazing. They are often caused by dust or oil. They may also result from air being trapped under the glaze of a too porous pot. Occasionally these occur because the kiln was fired too high too fast. Blisters may also form if one coat of glaze becomes too dry before the next is applied.

4. *Running*. If a commercially purchased glaze runs off the pot onto the kiln shelf during firing, the glaze was probably applied too thickly. Next time do not use as heavy an application of glaze. Be sure that the bottom third of your pot is glazed in a thinner layer if the glaze has a tendency to run heavily (true for many art glazes).

5. *Shivering*. Shivering is a defect where bits of glaze crack off the pot after firing. Its cause is the opposite of that for crazing. In crazing, the glaze shrinks more than the clay, causing the glaze to crack: Here the glaze coating is too small for the pot. In shivering the clay shrinks more than the glaze: Here the glaze coating is "too big" for the pot. The pressure of the excess glaze causes glaze pieces to crack off after firing. Both crazing and shivering are caused by improper fit of clay body and glaze. They can often be avoided by carefully choosing clays and glazes that complement each other.

Firing is the last step in the succession of processes that transform the shapeless blob into the finished bowl. The opening of the kiln door is the moment of truth in pottery. Here, the skill of the potter's hands and the interaction of clay and fire culminate at last in the finished form, irrevocably the sum of its parts. Successes have fused into harmonious wholes, while failures concretely and unrelentingly flaunt their flaws.

The clay has been wedged and shaped, the piece trimmed and decorated, bisqued, and finally glazed. Each of these processes influences the last step—what happens to the piece in the kiln. If the foregoing have been carefully executed and the kiln is now fired to the correct temperatures for the clay body and glaze, opening its door should be a little like the long-awaited arrival of Santa on the Christmas mornings of your childhood—exciting, full of surprises, replete with many treasures, and perhaps harboring a few disappointments. It is also a time of growth and learning in pottery—how to repeat your successes, how to avoid the same failures the next times. This is where the journal mentioned in the previous chapter can be very valuable for future reference. For better or worse, the pots are yours. There is nothing you can do at this point to change them.

In your initial pottery experiences, it is unlikely that you will be firing a kiln. Like the potter's wheel, it is an expensive investment that should not be undertaken because of an immediate and perhaps casual interest in creating clay ware. If you are taking a course in pottery, your pieces will be fired as part of the class experience. If you are working at home, there are many ceramic hobby shops that will fire your ware for a small fee. So a kiln of your own is not really necessary.

After you have made a true commitment to the craft of pottery, you may want to purchase a kiln

17

FIRING

yourself. With this in mind, in this chapter we will give a brief description of the processes involved in firing a kiln. Even if you never become involved in these processes yourself, you will have a better understanding of what happens when the clay is fired by learning something about kiln operation.

PROCESSES PRECEDING FIRING

As stated before, the firing of a pot is the culmination of all the steps that were part of its creation. If the clay was not properly wedged before being shaped, air trapped in the piece may cause it to crack, break, or even blow up in the kiln. If the piece was not thoroughly dried, the high heat of the kiln will turn excess water in the pot to steam, causing it to break or blow up. If the piece dried unevenly—for example, the handle of a cup dried faster than the cup—joined parts may fall off when the piece is fired. Small cracks or warpings in the dried piece will be accentuated in the firing. Improper glaze application may cause the piece to blister, crack, or craze. Improper fit of glaze to clay body may cause defects such as crazing or shivering. And, of course, if the clay is not fired to the correct temperatures, the pot may not be suitable for use. High-fire clays fired to low temperatures will be porous. Low-fire clays fired too high may melt. Firing temperatures will also affect glaze colors.

Firing is a most important step. Even if all the preceding procedures were executed with care, if the kiln is improperly fired, all your efforts will be wasted. A bad firing can ruin a kiln load of potentially beautiful pots.

KILNS—GENERAL INFORMATION

A kiln is essentially an oven designed for firing ceramics. Unlike your kitchen oven, it is capable of reaching very high temperatures. Even low-fire kilns commonly reach temperatures up to 2,000° F. Kilns may be heated by gas, electricity, wood, oil, or coal. The kilns most often used by home and hobby potters are electric. Some studio potteries and schools also use gas kilns. Electric kilns are generally smaller, simpler, and safer to operate than gas kilns. Gas kilns are often quite large, less expensive to run than electric kilns, generally fire to higher temperatures, and may be used for both oxidation- and reduction-firing. Both types of kiln have their advantages and disadvantages. The kiln's cost, ability to reach high temperatures, simplicity, and safety of operation and available space are some factors that influence the choice of kilns for different situations.

When you have reached the point of considering the purchase of a kiln of your own, visit your ceramic supply dealer and investigate the types of kilns available. You will probably choose an electric kiln for your first purchase in this area. Electric kilns take up little room, usually may be plugged into an ordinary wall socket, and require relatively short firing periods. Although many do not fire above earthenware temperatures, their range will prove suitable for most ceramic projects you will want to undertake.

There are some electric kilns that will fire at stoneware or even porcelain temperatures, but these are generally quite expensive. One limitation of an electric kiln is that it is suitable only for oxidation-firing. (It is possible but difficult to produce a reduction fire in an electric kiln.)

REDUCTION-FIRING

Although you may never own or operate a fuel-burning kiln, it may be possible for you to have

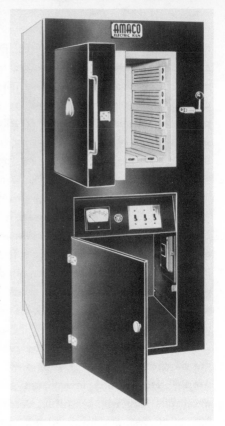

Electric front loading kiln. High fire kiln—fires to 2350 degrees. May be used for earthenware, stoneware, and porcelain. The chamber is 15 inches wide by 21 inches deep. (Photograph courtesy American Art Clay Company)

some pieces reduction-fired in a gas kiln if you are taking a ceramics course. Since reduction-firing is responsible for some very beautiful effects that are different from those produced by normal oxidation-firing, it is a process you should try if it is offered in your class.

Reduction-firing changes the colors of both clay and glazes by cutting down the oxygen supply in the kiln.

In oxidation or "regular" firing, more oxygen is present in the kiln than is needed for the clay and glazes to remain in their normal condition. Combustion takes place and allows the elements in ceramic materials to be completely oxidized. Most fired glazes and clay samples that you may look at when purchasing these materials were fired in an oxidation kiln. This is the usual manner of firing. In oxidation, oxygen is mixed with the fuel to produce a "clean" fire.

In reduction-firing, there is insufficient oxygen present in the kiln, complete combustion does not take place, and excess carbon is present. The carbon is "hungry" for oxygen and robs the clay and glazes of part of their oxygen content. This process, where ceramic materials are deprived of oxygen, is called reduction. It is achieved by denying the fire oxygen as the kiln is heated. A reduction fire is dirty, sooty, and smoky, as compared to an oxidation fire.

Reduction changes the color of both clays and glazes by pulling oxygen from them. For example, a clay that normally fires red will fire black in a reduction kiln, since reduction changes red iron oxide to black iron oxide. Red iron oxide, which normally produces beiges and browns in glazes, will cause these glazes to turn various shades of celadon green in a reduction-firing. Copper oxide, which usually produces blues and greens, turns red in a reduction-firing. These celadon green and copper red glazes are typical of reduction-firing.

Whether you use a small electric kiln or a large gas kiln, pottery is generally fired twice. The first, or bisque, firing turns the raw clay into a durable but still porous form. The second, or glost, firing is performed after the pot has been bisqued and glazed, and gives it its final decorative appearance as well as rendering it nonporous. The bisque-firing is usually lower in temperature than the glaze-firing. After bisquing the pot is no longer fragile but still porous enough to allow proper glaze adherence. When the ware is glaze-fired, the kiln is heated to the maturing temperatures of both clay and glazes.

CONES

A kiln reaches such high temperatures that it is impossible to measure its heat with an ordinary thermometer. Yet there must be some accurate way of determining the progress of firing. To do this, pyrometric (heat measuring) cones are used. These are small slender triangles, made from ceramic materials, which bend or deform at certain specified temperatures. Each cone has a specific number that corresponds to a certain temperature. For instance cone 06 (a common temperature at which low-fire earthenware matures) will bend between the temperatures of 1830° F. and 1870° F. Cone 010 (a low temperature for firing bisque ware) indicates a kiln temperature of 1640° F. to 1680° F.

Cones do not measure heat alone. Rather, they measure "work heat"—the combination of time and temperature that causes the clay and its glazes to mature. Pyrometric cones deform progressively as the temperatures within the kiln rise and so serve as accurate indicators of firing temperature. Three pyrometric cones, each of which matures at slightly varying temperatures, are generally used when firing a kiln. They are set at an angle of about 80° in a pat of clay or in a commercial cone-holder. The first, or lowest melting cone, serves as a warning signal that the kiln is almost ready to be shut off. The second deforms at the recommended firing

temperatures of the clay and glazes. It indicates that the ware has matured and the kiln should be turned off. The third bends at a still higher temperature and should not become deformed if the kiln is shut off at the proper time. For example, if you wish to fire your ware to cone 06, you would use three cones—06 to tell you when the ware is mature, 07 to indicate that the firing time is nearing its end, and cone 05, which would bend only if the kiln has been slightly overfired. These cones relate inversely to firing temperature—that is, cone 07 is a lower temperature than cone 05. Cones are numbered from cone 022 (the lowest temperature) to cone 01 (a higher temperature) and from cones 1 to 15. In cones 022 to 01, the lower the number the higher the heat. This inverse ratio holds true to cone 1. Then it reverses. Beginning with cone 1, the higher number indicates a higher temperature—that is, cone 2 temperature is hotter than cone 1, cone 5 hotter than cone 3.

All kilns have "peepholes" through which to observe the progression of the cones. Locate the cones in the kiln so that they may be easily watched through the peephole while the firing progresses.

Many electric kilns manufactured today may be purchased with an automatic "kiln sitter." This is a mechanical cut-off device that automatically shuts the kiln off when the proper temperatures have been reached. It eliminates the use of the clay pat with three cones and thus watching the progression of the cones in the kiln. Instead, one small cone of proper temperature measure (say cone 06 if that is your maturing temperature) is inserted horizontally to activate the kiln. When the proper temperature has been reached, the cone bends, releasing the switch, and the kiln shuts off automatically. Although a kiln sitter is an added expense, it is also a real convenience that greatly facilitates accurate firing for the beginner and that spares the experienced craftsman the task of constant kiln-watching. If you already have an electric kiln, a kiln sitter may be purchased separately and attached to the kiln.

KILN FURNITURE

The "furniture" of a kiln consists mainly of shelves and posts. The shelves or half-shelves are used to hold the pots as they are being fired. The posts, in varying sizes, support the shelves, allowing for the most efficient use of the space within the kiln. Other furniture consists of objects like stilts on which to place glazed pieces that should not touch the kiln shelf, firing racks for beads, and special stilts for firing jewelry.

When you buy a kiln, it is necessary to purchase at least one kiln shelf (preferably two or three, depending on the size of the kiln) and four posts to support the shelf (or about three or four posts per shelf). Other furniture may be acquired as the needs present themselves.

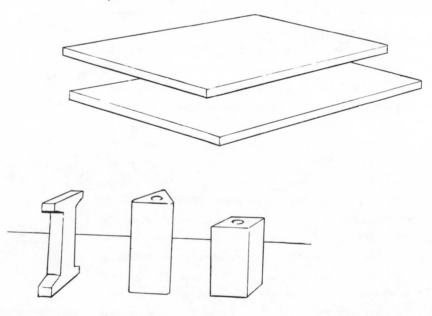

LOADING THE KILN

In firing bisque ware, the pieces may touch each other, as there is no glaze involved to fuse them together. In firing glazed ware, each piece must be placed far enough apart so that no two touch or they will stick together.

When firing the kiln, always try to make use of the space provided as efficiently as possible. In the bisque-firing, pieces should stand level on the kiln shelf to reduce warping. Smaller pots may be carefully stacked inside larger ones. A large bowl may hold a smaller bowl, and the small bowl a still smaller vase or piece of jewelry. When placing pieces inside each other, handle them with care and common sense. For example, do not place a small heavy piece inside a larger fragile piece with a thin bottom. Large shallow bowls or platters are best fired upside down to keep their rims from warping. Cups are often fired this way for the same reason. Always fire lidded pieces with their covers in place. Since the pieces in a bisque-firing may touch or be stacked within one another, it is possible to fire many more pots in this firing than the kiln will accommodate during the glaze-fire. Bisque ware is usually fired substantially lower than glaze ware—generally between cone 010 and cone 04.

Before glost-firing, the kiln shelves should be protected from stray glaze drippings with kiln wash. Kiln wash is used to coat shelves upon which the glazed pots will be placed. It prolongs the life of the shelves and makes it easy to remove glaze drippings that may run off the sides of the pieces. Kiln wash is sold in powdered form and mixed with water to thick cream consistency. It is painted onto the kiln shelves with a brush, using one or two heavy coats. Kiln wash may also be made by mixing equal parts of china clay powder and silica, adding these to water, and mixing to a heavy cream consistency. Paint on the kiln shelf as for commercially prepared kiln wash. It is not necessary to apply kiln wash each time a glaze load is fired. If some glaze drips onto the shelf, removal of these drippings will also mar the kiln wash in that area. To patch an area where the kiln wash has flaked off, simply apply one or two heavy coats to the marred surface as done when coating the entire shelf. A shelf may have several small patches before it is necessary to entirely recoat it.

When firing a glaze kiln, be sure to leave enough space between your pots so they do not touch each other; ¼ to ½ inch or more is advisable. All glaze should be cleaned off the foot of the pot at least ¼ inch from the base. If a pot is heavily glazed near the foot or requires some glaze on the bottom, it should be placed on "stilts" or triangles, small forms that keep the piece from touching the kiln shelves. Fire lidded pieces with covers, but be sure that there is no glaze in the areas where they touch.

FIRING BEADS

Ceramic beads that are glazed must be fired a special way to prevent them from fusing to the shelves of the kiln or to each other. Since beads are often glazed on all sides, there is no unglazed surface that can sit on the kiln shelf. Therefore, beads must be suspended on nichrome wire (a special heat-resistant wire), above the kiln shelf and apart from each other. There are two main variations of this process in firing glazed beads. (1) Buy a special bead rack at a ceramic supply shop. Although these vary slightly in design, they often consist of porcelain supports across which nichrome wires are placed horizontally. The beads are strung on the wires with sufficient distance between them so they

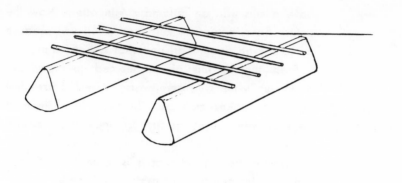

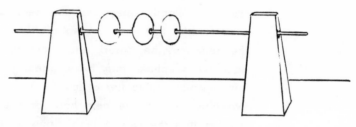

do not touch and there is no danger of their fusing together. The wires are placed across the supports, keeping the beads suspended above the kiln shelf. (2) Make two stable sturdy clay cones two to four inches high from a clay of your choice. Poke a hole through the top of each cone. Bisque-fire them. Attach nichrome wire through the hole of one cone. String the glazed beads on the wire, making sure they do not touch. Fasten the wire to the other cone, attaching it through the hole at the top. Place beads on holder in kiln and fire to proper temperature for clay and glaze maturation.

Nichrome wire may be purchased at a ceramic supply store or any shop that sells electric wire, such as a hardware store or hobby shop.

FIRING THE KILN

The kiln is stacked; the cones are in place so that they may be seen through the peephole (or you may have a kiln with an automatic kiln sitter). Now the actual firing begins. A kiln that is full will produce a more even firing than one that is half empty.

Even though the pieces seemed perfectly dry when put in the kiln, greenware or fresh glazes will hold atmospheric moisture. Therefore, the kiln must be fired very slowly at first to allow this moisture to evaporate.

Activate the kiln so that it is turned on. If your kiln has temperature controls, turn these to low. Allow the kiln to heat slowly. To ensure this, leave the door slightly open and the peepholes uncovered for the first hour or two of firing. After this, the door may be closed, and after about another hour, the peepholes may be plugged. Many electric kilns instruct you to fire at low for the first hour or two and medium the next hour or two and only then to turn the kiln to high, firing until the ware has reached maturity.

As the kiln progresses during the high firing cycle be sure to watch the cones regularly through the peephole. From the time the first cone bends, watch the progression of the second cone carefully to be sure the kiln does not overfire. When the second cone sags, it is time to turn off the kiln.

Allow the kiln to cool thoroughly. Generally a kiln takes at least as long to cool completely as it did to fire. So if your firing took six to eight hours, the kiln should be allowed the same amount of cooling time. If the kiln is opened too soon, the pieces may shatter or crack, harming the ware, the kiln, and you.

RAKU

While Raku is a total pottery process, it is included in this chapter because firing is the most unique aspect of its creation and the one that gives it most of its basic characteristics.

Raku is a pottery process developed by Oriental craftsmen around the sixteenth century for making ceremonial tea bowls. It is enjoying a new vogue among many potters today. Because of its short firing period (often as little as fifteen or twenty minutes) and unusual glaze effects, it is an exciting and immediately rewarding experience. Raku ware is distinguished by its interesting, often accidental glaze variation. Glazes tend to be quite glossy and often have a metallic luster. The clay ware remains porous and the glaze is not waterproof, and so the pieces are limited as far as functional use is concerned. However the decorative possibilities achieved in raku-firing are unique. Oxides sometimes provide rainbow-like colors to the glazed surface. Some pots develop deep crackle effects.

Whole books have been written on this one process. The purpose of these few pages will be only to give a brief overview of this very fascinating firing departure.

In the firing methods discussed previously, the glazed piece was placed in a cold kiln, the kiln heated slowly, the pieces allowed to fire to maturing temperature, and the kiln thoroughly cooled before the pot was removed. All these rules go out the window in firing raku. Here the glazed piece is placed in a hot kiln, fired for a short time until the glaze melts (often only fifteen or twenty minutes), immediately taken out and plunged into combustible materials such as sawdust, wood chips, or dry leaves to cause a reduction action in the glaze, and then cooled by dipping it into cold water. Long tongs are used to insert and remove the pot from the kiln, giving it the tong marks characteristic of this process.

The glaze-firing itself is quite dramatic, providing unusual effects in a minimum amount of time. In Japan the firing is generally done outdoors, often using a small charcoal-burning kiln. Many U.S. potters make raku kilns especially for this process. They are simple to construct, requiring only limited expenditures and materials. Often an old garbage can is lined with fire brick, and a gas blower is attached to supply the heat. Pots may also be fired in a small electric kiln. However there is something about an outdoor firing that captures the true spirit of raku—simplicity of form, quickness of firing, unusual and accidental glaze treatments.

It is not advisable to make a pot and decide at the last minute that you want to raku fire it. Although raku is basically a firing technique, other aspects of construction must be geared to this firing process in order to achieve the desired results. High-fire clay bodies, grog, certain methods of shaping, and special low-fire glazes are all necessary in constructing a raku pot.

Clay for making raku ware must be high-fire and porous enough to endure the sudden and extreme temperature shocks from hot to cold to which it will be subjected. Therefore a great deal of grog (30–40 percent) is added to the clay to increase porosity, and the piece is bisqued to around cone 04 so that it retains sufficient porosity even after firing. Since so much grog has been added, the clay will be less plastic than usual. This will limit your forms to rather simple structures. Hand-building methods such as pinching or simple and well-joined slab techniques are suitable, or the pot may be thrown on the wheel. (For throwing, add fine grog and decrease proportions added.) Coiling is not recommended for this process, since coils tend to break apart at their points of juncture. Keep all forms simple and walls a bit on the thick side.

Making Raku Pottery

MATERIALS

Heavily grogged stoneware or high-fire clay or special raku clay

Clear or colored transparent low-fire glazes or
   special raku glaze
Oxides or raku decorating colors, if desired
Raku tongs
Bucket or other container with tight-fitting lid. Fill
   half full with sand and place thick layer of
   combustible materials (such as sawdust) over
   sand
Bucket of cold water

Step 1: Make a simple shape from high-fire heavily grogged clay. Small bowls make good beginning projects.

Step 2: Fire the dry pot at a bisque temperature
of about cone 04.

Step 3: Apply clear or colored transparent low-fire
glazes or special raku glazes. Oxides may be applied under or over the glaze for added color
variations. Allow the glaze to dry completely.

Step 4: Heat the piece on top of the kiln, then
with tongs place the glazed piece directly into the
kiln, which has reached a temperature between
1600° and 1700° F. (cone 013 to cone 09). Use
either a small electric kiln or a raku kiln. Watch the
pot carefully, as this is a quick process.

Step 5. When the glaze appears red-hot and
shiny (about 1750° F., cone 08 or 09), remove the
piece with tongs. The glazed pot may now be treated
one of three ways.

Step 6: (a) Place the hot piece on a fireproof
surface and allow it to cool slightly. If the pot is a
closed form such as a vase or bottle, this step should
be observed before proceeding to the other steps
or the pot may crack. The piece may be air-cooled
entirely, without following up with b or c. (b) Lower
the piece carefully into a bucket or other large
container filled with sawdust, dry leaves, or other
such highly combustible material. Sometimes additional sawdust is thrown over the pot. Immediately

cover the bucket with a lid so that the action of
the smoking, smoldering glaze coming in contact
with the combustible materials in the container may
cause reduction to occur. Reduction occurs when
oxygen is cut off from the clay and glaze (due to
the lid being clamped on in this case), forcing
oxygen from the clay and glaze themselves. This
provides color changes in the metallic oxides. In
raku this produces some of the characteristic glaze
effects. After three or four minutes, the lid may
be removed and the pot plunged into cold water.
Or (c) remove the hot pot from the kiln and immediately plunge it into cold water for a minute or two.

Each of these treatments gives varying color
effects to the glazed raku pieces.

Raku platter. Vincent Rascone. Antonio Prieto Collection
of Modern Ceramics, Mills College. (Photograph by Margaret d'Hamer)

Epilogue

From your initial experiences in texturing and manipulation, from hand-building to throwing on the wheel, through glazing, decorating, and finally firing, this book has intended to expose you to enough basic skills and experiences within each area to provide you with a firm foundation in the rudiments of pottery. It is the hope of the author that these pages will serve only as a beginning from which you will go forward on your own, seeking out new experiences in this wide and varied craft. The projects listed in each section were meant to whet the appetite, not satisfy it; to show a small fraction of the possibilities of form, design, and imagination; to serve as a springboard for your own creations and to give you some direction while doing so. Many potters spend a lifetime exploring only a few aspects of this fascinating field.

Now that you have experienced in your own work the steps that actually are involved in changing the shapeless clay into the finished bowl, you will find that in this area these experiences have indeed affected your life. Obviously they have increased your awareness and appreciation of different sorts of pottery. Now when you see a ceramic form you will admire (or reject) it with the attitude of one who has himself experienced the medium, delighting in the fact that you know that it is a raku pot or has a sgraffito design. You will look at feet, lips, handles, notice joining of seams, or symmetry of form, admire technique or bemoan the lack of it. Your educated eye will view all pottery with more critical and knowledgeable insight. But it will not end there. You will go on to other books, explore other possibilities. You will find at the seashore and in the woods not only solitude and renewal, but an endless treasure chest of texturing devices, shells and fossils, bark and pods, stones and bones. And you may save them not only as mementos, as you once did, but as tools of your craft. As you pick up that special shell or rock, you will find that clay has subtly crept in, broadening your awareness of nature, opening you to see details and nuances that you might have missed before. Or you may find yourself looking at gadgets in the kitchen section of the supermarket or hardware store, seeing them not as objects to perform the function for which they were intended, but wondering instead how that meat tenderizer would print on wet clay.

This is not to say, of course, that your life will revolve around pottery. Some of you may choose it as an enduring and satisfying hobby, a vehicle for exploring your own creative urges and a method for surrounding yourself with inexpensive, beautiful, and unique handmade products that are extensions of your own talents. Lack of time or precedence of other interests may keep others only minimally or sporadically involved with clay. But even if your experiences in this area will be limited, your very involvement in it at all has already provided you with a permanent change of vision. If, for a few of you, ceramics speaks the language of your soul and becomes a major commitment, there is of course no end to the many-branched road that you can travel in this field.

As the Creator, according to the Bible, blew His breath into clay to form man, investing him with some of His own attributes, man, in his turn, has "blown his breath" into clay, adding something of himself, giving form and beauty to shapeless earth. Pottery-making is somehow a symbol of the nature of man, a creature tied by his physical limitations to the soil on which he dwells but whose spiritual wings lift him above the other beasts with whom he shares his domain. Working in clay is a synthesis of these two essential aspects—the eternal quality of man's relationship to earth with the expression of his own creative forces.

That inner spirit of creation that transcends time and culture lives within each of us. The spark exists, whether it is ignited ·by music, poetry, painting, pottery, or whatever vehicle we choose to give it expression. It is the hope of the author that this book has fed that spark within you, has helped to open a new door wide enough to intrigue you with what lies beyond and that the experiences it has provided have given you pleasure.

Glossary

Air bubbles: Pockets of air trapped in the clay. These are often left by inadequate wedging. They are undesirable and may result in flawed work.

Banding wheel (or bench wheel): A round turntable on which hand-built pottery may be constructed or on which forms are decorated or glazed.

Bat: A plaster disc or slab on which pottery is formed or dried.

Bisque (or biscuit) firing: The first firing, which hardens the clay before it is glazed.

Bisque (or biscuit) ware: Unglazed clay ware that has been fired once.

Blistering: A glaze defect where bubbles appear on the glazed pot. May be caused by overrapid firing or dust or oil left on the surface of a bisqued pot.

Bone dry: Very dry clay, ready for firing.

Casting: The process of pouring slip into plaster molds to create pieces in the shape of the mold.

Centering: The first step in throwing on the wheel. Getting the clay exactly in the center of the wheel-head.

Clay: A plastic body consisting of fine particles of decomposed granite or other feldspathic rock.

Clay body: A mixture of natural clays and other ceramic materials blended to make a more predictable and easier-to-work-with product. Earthenware, stoneware, and porcelain are the most common clay bodies.

Coil pot: A form made by rolling out ropes of clay and layering them on top of one another.

Collaring: A method of narrowing the neck of a thrown form by squeezing or pressing in with both hands.

Cones: Small slender triangles of ceramic material that bend or melt at specific kiln temperatures. Their bend-ing indicates that the clay and glazes have been fired to maturity.

Crawling: A glaze defect that causes the glaze to separate into clumps or patches during firing, leaving some areas of the form unglazed. Crawling is often caused by too heavy glaze application, which cracks upon drying.

Crazing: A glaze defect that causes the glaze to crackle undesirably. It may occur when the clay body and glaze do not fit each other.

Dipping: A method of glazing where the pot is immersed in a large quantity of glaze.

Earthenware: Low-fire pottery.

Egyptian paste: A self-glazing low-fire ceramic body invented in ancient Egypt, used primarily in making jewelry or other miniature forms.

Engobe: White or colored slip used to decorate clay ware.

Firing: The process of heating clay ware to specific temperatures in a kiln.

Firing range: The span between the highest and lowest temperatures at which a clay body or glaze may be fired to maturity.

Flux: The lowest melting compound in a glaze. It combines easily with silica and alumina to lower the melting point of the glaze.

Fly wheel: The part of the potter's wheel that is kicked to control the speed of the wheel.

Foot: The base of a ceramic piece.

Frit: A material used in glazes made from melted cooled glass that has been ground to powder.

Glaze: A glasslike coating that fuses to the clay body in firing. It serves to make the piece watertight and to decorate it.

Glaze or glost firing: The second firing in which the kiln is fired to the temperature at which the glaze matures.

Greenware: Clay that has not been fired.

Grog: Ground bisqued clay that is added to a clay body to reduce shrinkage and warping and to add texture.

Kiln: A furnace in which pottery pieces are fired.

Kiln furniture: Shelves and posts on which ceramic pieces are placed when they are fired in the kiln.

Kiln sitter: A device that automatically shuts off the kiln when it has reached the proper temperature.

Kiln wash: A protective coating that is made from china clay and silica and that is painted onto kiln shelves .and floors to allow for easy removal of glaze drippings.

Leather-hard: Clay that has dried to a stage where it is no longer pliable but still soft enough to carve, damp but firm.

Oxidation-firing: Regular firing with sufficient oxygen present in the kiln for clay and glazes to remain in their normal condition.

Oxides: Metallic chemicals that are used for adding color to glazes, slips, and clay bodies.

Peephole: An opening in the kiln wall or door for viewing the progression of the cones (and therefore the progression of firing).

Pinch pot: A clay form made by pinching the clay and squeezing it between the fingers.

Plasticity: That attribute of clay that allows it to be worked on and shaped without breaking; its "molding" property.

Potter's wheel: A rotating wheel on which pots are thrown. A machine that is operated either by foot or by electric power and that speeds up and facilitates the shaping of round symmetrical clay ware.

Primary (residual) clay: Natural clay found in pockets in its original area of formation.

Pyrometric: Heat-measuring (as in pyrometric cones, pyrometers, and other devices used to measure the heat of the kiln).

Raku: A pottery method developed in Japan that utilizes high-fire heavily grogged clay, low-fire glazes, and a rapid firing and cooling process.

Reduction: A type of firing with reduced oxygen present in the kiln that causes a change in clay and glaze colors.

Ribs: Wooden, metal, or rubber tools used for finishing pottery. May be used to smooth the inside of a bowl or as an aid in throwing pottery.

Score: To scratch a moist piece of clay with a sharp tool before joining it to another clay piece. The clay is scratched in one direction and then the other. Slip is applied to the scratchings and the pieces are pressed together.

Secondary (sedimentary) clay: Clay that has been transported by the elements from its original site of formation.

Sgraffito: A decorating technique in which a sharp tool is used to scratch through slip or glaze to expose the clay body or the background color.

Slake: To moisten clay with water.

Slip: Clay mixed with water to about the consistency of thick cream.

Slip trailing: A decorating technique where colored slip is placed in a syringe or squeeze bottle and trailed or squirted in a design on a clay surface.

Stoneware: A high fire nonporous clay body. Generally buff or gray in color.

Template: A pattern placed against the sides of a clay form that serves as a guide in shaping the piece.

Throw: To make pottery on the potter's wheel.

Vitrify: To turn into glass or become glasslike.

Wax resist: A decorating technique where wax is painted on a pot. Glaze is brushed over the wax. The wax repels the glaze. Wax may also be painted on greenware, and engobe brushed over the wax. The wax repels the engobe.

Wedging: The process of getting air bubbles out of the clay and making it uniform in consistency.

Wheel: Another term for potter's wheel.

Wheel-head: That part of the potter's wheel on which the clay is formed.

Index

Accoutrements, 152–162
  casserole (inset lid), 157–158
  handles, 152–156
    steps for pulling, 153–155
    variations in, 155–156
  knobs, 158–160
  lidded piece, 157
  lips on a pitcher, 156
  spouts, 160–162
Acrylic paint, 121
Air bubbles, 131, 228
  wedging and, 31, 32, 33
Aluminum, 17, 181
Animals, pinch pot, 71–73
  small turtle, 72–73
Appliqués, 173
Ashtrays, 62, 63–64

Bailey, Clayton, 59, 103, 105
Ball clay, 18
Banding wheel (bench wheel), 30, 228
Bats, 28, 132, 228
Beads, 43–45
  firing, 218–219
Beasley, Bruce, 43
Bells, 66–68
Belly, forming a, 144, 145
Bench wheel (banding wheel), 30, 228
Bentonite, 18, 23
Bible, 226–227
Bisque (biscuit) firing, 39, 179, 228
  for throwing, 135
Bisque (biscuit) ware, 39, 228
Blistering, 208, 228
Bohn, Diana, 83, 115
Bone dry, 228
Bottles, 144–148
  making, 144–146
  trimming, 146–148
  used as molds, 118–120

Bowls, 143–144
  coil method, 79–82
  pinch pot technique, 62, 63
Boxes, slab pot, 95–98
Brick-making, 15
Brushes for glazing, 29
Brushing the glaze, 187–189
Bunker, Eugene, 176
Bursak, Judy, 162, 196
Buttons, 45–46

Carving, 172–173
Casserole (inset lid), 157–158
Casting, 228
Centering, 133, 228
  for throwing, 135
Ceramics art or craft, 15
Chamois leather, 132
China, ancient, 127
China clay powder, 217–218
Chromium, 181
Chuck (concave cylinder), 147, 148
Clay, 228
  buying, 24–26
    from reputable dealer, 24
    slip (liquid form), 25
    things to consider, 26
    wet or dry form, 24
  digging your own, 21–23
    steps in, 22–23
  geological source of, 16–17
  as a medium, 11, 15–20
  nature of, 15–16
  prehistoric uses of, 1
  types of , 17–18
Clay body, 18–20, 228
  compared to natural clay, 18–19
  See also Earthenware; Porcelain;
    Stoneware
Clay tablets, 2

Coating, slip decoration, 174
Cobalt, 181
Coil pots, 74–86, 228
    basic form: cylinders, 76–79
    bowls, 79–82
        do-it-yourself molds, 115–117
    joining, 75
    large pots, 83–84
    pieces with handles, 84–86
    size and thickness, 75
    surface texture, 74–75
    templates, 81
    vases, 79–82
Cole, Michele, 64, 91, 170, 171
Collaring, 139–140, 228
Cones, 214–216, 228–229
Containers, using, 28
Cookie-cutter Christmas tree ornaments, 125–126
Copper oxide, 181, 213
Cracking defect, 183, 207
Crawling defect, 207–208, 229
Crazing defect, 183, 207, 229
Cutting wire (tool), 28, 132
Cylinders
    coil method, 76–79
    throwing, 136–140
        basic form, 133
        bottle shape, 144–146

Decoration, 193–207
    Egyptian paste, 203–207
    engobes, 194
    frit, 199–200
    glaze, 193–207
    lusters, 200–203
    oxides or stains, 197–199
    pre-firing, 168–180
        on dry clay, 179–180
        leather-hard clay processes, 172–178
        things to consider, 168–169
        wet clay processes, 169–172
    sgraffito, 194–195
    wax resist, 195–197
Dental tools, 173
Dipping the glaze, 191–192, 229
Dowel rod technique, 102–105
Dry clay
    decorating on, 179–180
    mixing, 30–31
Dry clay
    decorating on, 179–180
    mixing, 30–31

Drying time, 37–39
    air circulation, 37–38
    shrinkage and, 39
    stages of, 38–39
    for throwing, 135

Earrings, 47–49
Earthenware, 18, 229
    glazing, 19
    kiln temperatures, 39
    working with, 19
Egypt, ancient, 2, 127, 203
Egyptian paste, 203–207, 229
    how to make, 204–207
Elasticlay, 121
Electric kilns, operating costs, 211
Electric wheel, 128–129
Elephant ear sponge, 28, 132
Engobe, 174–176, 229
    glaze decoration, 194
    raw, 176
    slip decoration, 174–176
Entemena, King, 7
Exercises, 40–42
    manipulation, 40
    texture, 41–42

Faience, 2, 203
    See also Egyptian paste
Fairbanks, Richard, 42
Feldspar, 17
Fettling knife, 29
Fire clay, 18
Firing, 39, 209–224, 229
    activating processes, 219–220
    general information, 210–211
    processes preceding, 210
    purpose of, 121
Firing range, 26, 229
Flanged lids, 157
Flaws in the glaze, 207–208
Flux, 17, 229
    function of, 181
Fly wheel, 128, 229
Foot, 229
Free-form constructions, slab work, 98–102
Frit, 199–200, 229

Garden goblins, 69–71
Gas kilns, operating costs, 211
Glass-making, 15
Glaze and glazing, 39, 181–208, 229
    brushes for, 29

colors, 181
  commercial availability, 182–183
  firing temperature and, 210
  oxide applied over, 198–199
  in reduction-firing, 213
commercial, 29–30, 182–183
common flaws in, 207–208
composition of, 181–182
decorating techniques, 193–207
  Egyptian paste, 203–207
  engobes, 194
  frit, 199–200
  lusters, 200–203
  oxides or stains, 197–199
  sgraffito, 194–195
  wax resist, 195–197
discovery of, 2
function of, 181
how to choose, 183–185
methods of, 187–193
  brushing, 187–189
  dipping, 191–192
  pouring, 189–191
  spraying, 192–193
Raku pottery, 221, 224
slip decoration, 175
steps preceding, 186–187
test tiles, 185–186
for throwing, 135
Glost (second glaze firing), 181, 217, 229
Greece, ancient, 127
Greenware, 39, 229
Grog, 18, 131, 222, 229
  functional purpose of, 36
  for slab-building, 88
  as a texturing device, 36–37
Ground glass (frit), 199–200, 229
Grundler, Anni, 45, 47, 56, 71, 79, 112, 179

Handles, 84–86
  for a coil pot, 85–86
  pulling, 152–156
    steps in, 153–155
    variations in, 155–156
Hanging pieces, 56–58
Hanging planter, do-it-yourself molds, 115–117
Hanging weed pot, 107–109
Hotek, Ron, 171

Impressed decorations, 170–171
Inset lid, 157

Iron oxide, 198–199

Japan, Raku glaze-firing in, 221
Jewelry, 47–51

Kaolin, 18
Kaufman, Deborah, 84
Kick wheel, 128, 129
Kiln, 27, 229
  cooling time, 220
  firing, 209–224, 229
    activating process, 219–220
    beads, 218–219
    cones and, 214–216
    general information, 210–211
    and glazing temperatures, 39
    lidded pieces, 218
    loading for, 217–218
    processes preceding, 210
    Raku pottery, 220–222
    range, 26, 229
    reduction-, 211–213
  peepholes, 215, 230
  space considerations, 217, 218
  types of, 210–211
Kiln furniture, 216, 229
Kiln sitter, 215–216, 230
Kiln wash, 217–218, 230
King, Peggy, 173, 199, 202
Kneading clay, 32–33
Knobs, 158–160
Kranz, Vera, 66

Large pots, coil method, 83–84
Latex paint, 121
Lead oxides, 181, 184–185
Leather-hard, 132, 230
  decorative processes (pre-firing),172–178
    appliqués, 173
    carving, 172–173
    sgraffito, 178
    slip decoration, 174–176
    slip trailing, 176–177
  in slab-building, 88–89
Lid throwing, 157
  casserole (inset lid), 157–158
Lidded pieces, firing, 218
Lips, 149
  on a pitcher, 156
Luster decoration, 200–203

Macramé decoration, 179, 180
Manganese, 181

Manipulation, exercises in, 40
Marble-X, 121
Mask, three-dimensional, 110–112
Materials, 28–30
    for potter's wheel, 132
    See also names of materials
Metal rib, 29, 132
Metallic oxides, 181
Mexican Pottery Clay, 121
Mixing bowls, used as molds, 115–117
Mobiles and wind chimes, 56–58
Molds, do-it-yourself, 106–120
    forms and shape, 107
    possibilities to explore, 106
    using bottles, 118–120
    using mixing bowls, 115–117
    using newspapers, 107–112
    using oatmeal boxes, 114–115
    using paper tubes, 112–114

Necklaces, 49–51
Needle
    for testing thickness, 28
    for trimming, 132
Newspapers, used as molds, 107–112
    hanging weed pot, 107–109
    three-dimensional mask, 110–112
Nichrome wire, 218, 219
Non-fire clay, 121–126
    cookie-cutter Christmas tree ornaments, 125–126
    oven-fire products, 122–124
        steps used in, 123–124
    painting, 121, 122
    self-hardening products, 124–125
    variations of, 121–122

Oatmeal boxes, used as molds, 114–115
Oestreich, Donna, 108
"Off the hump" throwing technique, 150–151
Oilcloth material, 28
Opening, for throwing, 135
Oven-firing clays, 122–124
    steps used in, 123–124
Owl, wheel-thrown, 163–164
Oxidation-firing, 212–213, 230
Oxides, 174, 181, 221, 230
    glaze decoration, 197–199

Paddling with a board, 163
Painting slip decoration, 174–176
Paper tubes, used as molds, 112–114

Peephole, 215, 230
Pendants, 47–49
Picasso, Pablo, 175
Pierce, Linda, 63
Piggy bank, thrown, 165–166
Pinch pot, 59–73, 230
    animal shapes, 71–73
        small turtle, 72–73
    ashtrays, 62–65
    basic steps, 60–62
    bells, 66–68
    bowls, 62–65
    clay used for, 60
    for different sizes, 59–60
    garden goblins, 69–71
    vases, 62–65
Pinching a wet piece, 163
Pinholes (glaze defect), 208
Pins, 47–49
Pitchers, making, 156
Plaster bats, 28
Plastic clay, 18
Plasticity, 16, 230
Plates (soft slab method), 89–90
Platters (soft slab method), 91–93
Polycraft, 121
Polyform, 121
Porcelain, 18, 19
    kiln temperatures, 39
Potter's wheel, 27, 127–151, 230
    discovery of, 2, 127–128
    general information, 127–131
    learning to operate, 130–131
    for left-handed person, 129–130
    for right-handed person, 129
    types of wheels in use, 128–129
    See also Thrown pieces
Pottery
    in ancient times, 1–14
    compared to ceramics, 15
    defined, 15
Pouring the glaze, 189–191
Preparing the clay, 30–31
Prieto, Antonio, 198, 201
Primary (residual) clay, 17, 230
Pulling handles, 152–156
Pulling up, for throwing, 135
Pyrometric cones, 214–216, 230

Raku, 220–224, 230
    clay for, 222
    firing methods, 220–222
    glazes, 221, 224

making pottery, 222–224
Rascone, Vincent, 224
Raw engobes, 176
Reconditioning the clay, 35
Reduction-firing, 211–213, 230
Ribs, 29, 132, 230
Rims, making, 149
Robert Brent's Potter's Wheels, 128
Rubber (tool), 29
Rubber ear syringe, 177
Rubber kidney (tool), 29, 132
Running (glaze defect), 208

Sand, 18
Scheier, Edwin, 178
Score, 230–231
Sculpey, 121
Secondary (sedimentary) clay, 17, 231
Sectional constructions, thrown pieces, 166–167
Self-hardening clays, 124–125
Sgraffito, 178, 231
  glaze decoration, 194–195
Shaping for throwing, 135
Shivering defect, 183, 208
Shrinkage, 15, 16
  reducing, 36
  while drying, 39
Silica, 17, 217–218
  function of, 181
Simple projects, 43–58
  beads, 43–45
  buttons, 45–46
  hanging pieces, 56–58
  jewelry, 47–51
    necklaces, 49–51
    pendants, pins, and earrings, 47–49
  tiles, 51–54
  trivets, 55
Slab pots, 87–105
  boxes, 95–98
  dowel rod technique, 102–105
  free-form construction, 98–102
  leather-hard construction, 88–89
  rolling practice, 88
  sling pieces—platter (soft method), 91–95
  soft slab construction, 88–89
  trays or plates (soft method), 89–90
  use of grog, 88
  varieties of construction, 87–89
Slake, 231
Sling pieces (soft slab method), 93–95

Slip, 25, 231
Slip decoration, 174–176
  coating, 174
  painting, 174–176
Slip trailing, 176–177, 231
Small turtle, pinch pot, 72–73
Somerville, Joanne, 43, 47
Sponge materials, 28, 132
Spouts, 160–162
Spraying the glaze, 192–193
Squeezing with fingers, 163
Stains, glaze decoration, 197–199
Stilts, 218
Stoneware, 18, 231
  glazing, 20
  kiln temperatures, 39
  working with, 20
Storage, 35–36
Sumerians, ancient, 2, 127

Tempera paint, 121
Template, 81, 231
Test tiles, how to use, 185–186
Texture
  in coil building, 74–75
  exercises in, 41–42
  grogged clay, 36–37
  impressed decorations, 170–171
Thompson, Andrée, 47, 95
Three-dimensional mask, 110–112
Throwing, 231
  accoutrements, 152–162
  basic tips for, 133–135
  bottle shape, 144–146
  bowl, 143–144
  centering, 133, 228
  clay for, 131–132
  cylinder, 136–140
  lips and rims, 149
  "off the hump," 150–151
  steps to follow, 135
  tall vase, 144–146
  trimming, 141–143
    bottle, 146–148
  variations, 163–167
    owl, 163–164
    piggy bank, 165–166
    sectional constructions, 166–167
  working quickly with, 135
  See also Potter's wheel
Tile-making, 15
Tiles, 51–54

Tools
    basic materials, 28–30
    hands and fingers, 27
    for pottery wheel, 132
Tracing (slip trailing), 176–177, 231
Trays (soft slab method), 89–90
Trimming, 135, 141–143
    bottles, 146–148
Trimming tool, 29
Trimmings, 35
Trivets, 55
Turntable, 30

Variations, wheel form, 163–167
Vases
    coil method, 79–82
    pinch pot, 62, 64–65
    throwing, 144–146
Vitrify, 231
Voulkas, Peter, 196

Water-base paint, 121

Wax resist, 231
    commercially prepared, 186–187
    glaze decoration, 195–197
Wedging, 31–34, 231
    methods, 32–33, 34
    using grog with, 36–37
Wedging board, 32
Wedging table, 32
Wet clay, pre-firing decorative process,
        169–172
    adding clay, 172
    impressed decorations, 170–171
Wheel, 2, 231
Wheel-head, 231
Wind chimes, 56–58
Wire loop tool, 29
Wire trimming tool, 132
Wooden kidney tool, 29
Wooden modeling tool, 28
Wooden rib, 132

Zimmerman, Michi, 41, 51, 89, 99, 118